DATE DUE

DEC 3 0 99		

DEMCO 38-296

THE CURIOUS HISTORIES
OF PLACE-NAMES

Derek Nelson

 KODANSHA INTERNATIONAL
New York • Tokyo • London

Kodansha America, Inc.
114 Fifth Avenue, New York, New York 10011, U.S.A.

Kodansha International Ltd.
17-14 Otowa 1-chome, Bunkyo-ku, Tokyo 112, Japan

Published in 1997 by Kodansha America, Inc.

Library of Congress Cataloging-in-Publication Data
Nelson, Derek, 1950–
    Off the map : the curious histories of place-names / Derek Nelson.
        p.   cm.
    Includes bibliographical references (p.   ) and index.
    ISBN 1-56836-174-2
    1. Names, Geographical.   I. Title.
    G104.5.N45   1997
    910'.3—dc21   *97-25499*
                                                                   CIP

Book design by Adrianne Onderdonk Dudden

Manufactured in the United States of America

    98 99 00 QBP 10 9 8 7 6 5 4 3 2

CONTENTS

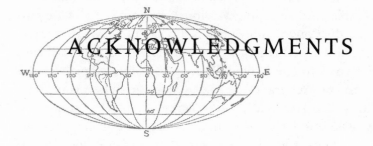

ACKNOWLEDGMENTS

As with my other books, I first want to express my deepest thanks to my wife, Mary, and my son, Nate. Their encouragement, support, and tolerance were crucial.

My editor, Deborah Baker (joined later by her assistant, Alexandra Babanskyj), ranged far beyond the call of duty in helping me corral and hog-tie a subject that careened through centuries and across continents. Her guidance was consistently constructive.

Randy Flynn, Executive Secretary for Foreign Names at the Defense Mapping Agency, was particularly helpful and patient in answering my questions and handling my requests.

The following people lent their insight, experience, and knowledge to the book. I have listed them not in order of the magnitude of their contributions but in the usual alphabetic style:

Pengiran Basmillah Abbas, First Secretary, Permanent Mission of Brunei Darussalam to the United Nations; Daniel Abibi, Ambassador, Mission Permanente de la République du Congo Aupres des Nations Unies; Adam Adawa, staff of the Permanent Representative, Permanent Mission of Kenya to the United Nations; Caroline Appiah of the Consulate-General of Ghana; Ayden Beyazit-Guvenc, Secretary, Permanent Mission of Turkey to the United Nations; Jan-Olov Bojarp, Ostersund, Sweden; Carolyn Bowler, Idaho State Historical Society, Boise, Idaho; John Broderick, Ph.D., Old Dominion University; David Broecker, Basel, Switzerland; Melchiade Bukuru, Chargé d'Affaires, Mission Permanente de la République du Burundi; staff of the Consulado General de Chile, New York; Delia Chatoor, staff of the Chargé d'Affaires, Trinidad and Tobago Mission to the United Nations; Jeremy Crampton, Ph.D., Professor of Cartography, George Mason University; C. M. Dlamini, staff of the Permanent Mission of the Kingdom of Swaziland to the United Nations; Michael Dobson, Ph.D., chief cartographer, Rand McNally; Hank Doyle, Public Relations, Rand McNally; staff of the Consulate General of Estonia; Susan Frydendahl, Greenland Home Rule, Denmark Office; Iris Geddis, staff of the Permanent Representative to the United Nations for Singapore; staff of the German Information Center of New York; Elisabeth Halvarsson-Stapen, Swedish Information Service; Hilary Harker, Librarian, Permanent Mission of Jamaica to the United Nations; Bodil Hartman, Information Officer, Royal Danish Consulate General; Anita Lisbey, Belize Archives Department, Belmopan, Belize; F. Veronica Lowe, Bermuda Department of Tourism; Kriesnadath Nandoe, Ambassador, Permanent Mission of Suriname to the United Nations; Glenn Nelson,

ACKNOWLEDGMENTS

my father, particularly for handy translation services in two languages, German and Japanese; Julie Naulls, Public Affairs Office, New Zealand Embassy; Awa Ouedraogo, Counsellor, Chargé d'Affaires, Burkina Faso; Mohan Panday, Consul General, Royal Nepalese Consulate General; Kings M. Phiri, Head, History Department, University of Malawi; M. V. L. Phiri, staff of the Ambassador, Permanent Mission of the Republic of Malawi to the United Nations; Miklos Pinther, Chief, Cartographic Section, Department of Public Information at the United Nations; Jovanka Ristic, Reference Librarian, American Geographical Society Collection at the University of Wisconsin-Milwaukee Library; George Sakamoto, Tokyo; Maria P. Sgro, Attaché, Misión Permanente de Panamá ante las Naciones Unidas; Don Smith, Ph.D., Department of Sociology and Criminal Justice, Old Dominion University; Per Sommer, Royal Danish Embassy, Washington, D.C.; Raymond C. Taylor, Chargé d'Affaires, Permanent Mission of St. Kitts and Nevis; Nirmal Tuladhar, Managing Editor, Contributions to Nepalese Studies, Research Centre for Nepal & Asian Studies; Juan José Valdés, National Geographic Society; Jean Winters, Kuwait Information Office, Embassy of the State of Kuwait; Maria Zoupaniotis, Press Counsellor, Permanent Mission of the Republic of Cyprus to the United Nations; and Felipe Zobaran, Editor-Chefe, Editora Azul S.A., Sao Paulo, Brazil.

ACKNOWLEDGMENTS

Fig. 1. Some early cartographers filled in the blank spaces on their maps with fanciful creations; others were more forthright about the limits of their knowledge, designating such areas as the "Terre Incognue" (land unknown) at the bottom of this 1646 French map, or the region optimistically labeled "Pays non Encore Descouverts" (country not yet discovered) at the top. (Reproduced from the collections of the Library of Congress.)

WELCOME
TO TERRA INCOGNITA

Cartography is 20 percent geography and science and 80 percent ignorance, myth, and greed—the arbitrary, impulsive, and ironic, snarled in history and politics. Maps contain tragedy, humor, and beauty, too, if you dig beneath the surface. When most people look at maps, however, they see pure geography. The thick lines marking national boundaries and the place-names, printed in dark type, seem proper and unchangeable, brooking no questions or investigation. Maps seem definite and fact-filled; few mark border disputes with dotted lines, symbols of impermanence. Maps lack the probablys and maybes that journalists find handy.

I never realized how important these qualifiers were. I used to look up something in my atlas, find the answer, and put the book back on the shelf. Several years ago some friends moved to County Westmeath in Ireland. Where is it? It is in the east central part of the country, 50 miles north of Dublin, 6 degrees west longitude and 53 degrees north latitude. Case closed. Ireland is Ireland, right? Well, not exactly. The location and boundaries are clear, but the name is more complex. Some people in Ireland don't say "Ireland"; they say "Eire," the Gaelic version and, according to the country's 1937 constitution, its official name. They have a Gaelic name for Dublin, too, although, ironically, the name of the capital was not a foreign imposition to start with, simply the last part of a long Gaelic name, Baile Atha Cliath Dubh Lind, meaning "town on the ford of hurdles on the black water" (farmers put wooden hurdles in shallow water to help animals across). Dublin had been headquarters of Viking invaders, then of Danish occupiers from the ninth to the twelfth centuries (they called it Divelin), and later of English invaders. Those for whom the name Dublin conjured too many associations with foreign domination prefer using the first three words of the Gaelic name (pronounced "bla-klee'-o"), which lacks this taint.

A nation's identity is wrapped up in its place-names, which mark the presence and history of a people. Not every national boundary is like the Red Sea, geographically fixed. Hundreds are disputed, each one triggering cartographic duels between mapmakers. Japanese maps show old Japanese names for some of the Kurile Islands, now occupied and claimed by Russia, whose maps, of course, show Russian names.

Is it Ivory Coast or Côte d'Ivoire? Burma or Myanmar? Governments disagree and international maps are inconsistent. "Happy the land that has a name truly related to its history, euphonious and easy in use, unambiguous, and giving offence to none," writes C. M. Matthews, whose

Place-Names of the English-Speaking World is a standard reference in the field. Canada is one of the lucky few. Its name, used by indigenous people before Europeans arrived, appeared as early as the 1550s on a map of the explorations made by Jacques Cartier in the Saint Lawrence Basin during the previous two decades. "Canada" designated parts of the region north of the Saint Lawrence. Its meaning, from the Iroquois *kanata*, "collection of huts," isn't grandiose, but it is long-lived and apparently offends no one—and therefore it is exceptional. Controversy is the norm.

A young woman named Janet cuts my hair. Her mother was born in Japan, her father in America, where Janet was born and raised. When Janet's Japanese cousins visit and she says the name Japan in conversation, it irritates them. They feel that she should know that the real name is Nippon. We got the name Japan from the Chinese (it means "land of the rising sun" in both languages). How many other countries use names that are different from the English version? What do the names mean, and where did they come from?

Sometimes explorers bestowed descriptive names; Hong Kong is Mandarin for "favorable water" or "fragrant harbor." Columbus named islands after the particular day of the week he sighted land. Sailing past Waitukubuli (tail of her body) on a Sunday, he called it Dominica (now the Commonwealth of Dominica). James Cook christened places after the distant royalty who funded his expeditions. Mapmakers rarely lived in the lands they mapped. Sometimes their source of information about boundaries and place-names came from those staking claims and establishing empires, factors that skewed cartography.

New maps are invariably based on old maps, and many country names predate the Middle Ages, an era when the courage and persistence of explorers far exceeded their knowledge. They worked, in the words of R. A. Skelton, a prominent cartographic historian and curator of the British Museum's map room, at "the uncertain boundary between knowledge and ignorance." Early medieval cartography, which derived in roughly equal parts from mythology and Babylonian cadastral maps (land surveys on clay tablets, dating from 2000 B.C.), was more superstitious than scientific; mapmakers readily accepted thirdhand accounts of giants in South America and Edenic islands in the North Atlantic.

Beginning in the thirteenth century, though, observation and measurement began to prevail, first in nautical charts—notably, Italian portolan charts, executed on parchment—and several hundred years later, in land maps. The first modern terrestrial globe made its appearance in 1492, the joint creation of a cosmographer and a miniaturist. The role of politics in geography grew seemingly in direct proportion to mapmakers' and explorers' expanding knowledge of the world.

Even before mapmakers choose place-names, they must answer two simple questions: on a flattened view of the globe (called a projection), what is the center of the world, and what shape are the continents? For Homer and the ancient Greeks, Greece was in the middle, surrounded by a huge river they called Oceanus. They considered the city of Delphi, near the foot of the south slope of Mount Parnassus, to be the heart of the inhabited world. It was the seat of ancient Greece's most famous and powerful oracle.

In some ancient Indian cosmographies, Mount Kailas in Tibet was the center of the world. Hindus believed this 22,000-foot peak to be sacred; Sanskrit literature described it as the paradise of Siva, god of destruction and birth.

Other Indian maps centered at Varanasi, formerly Benares, in Uttar Pradesh State in north central India on the Ganges River. It is the holiest city of the Hindus, as well as one of the world's oldest cities, with 1,500 temples, palaces, and shrines. Hindus believe that dying there releases them from the cycle of rebirth and allows them to enter heaven. An ancient Indian observatory at Ujjain was also used as a central meridian on maps.

During his twenty-two years of journeying through Asia and living in China in the late 1200s, Marco Polo used Arab maps that had north at the bottom. Some British maps, such as the one Sir Walter Raleigh used in his search for El Dorado, did the same. Medieval mapmakers in Europe usually put the east (where the rising sun symbolized the "risen Christ") on top and Jerusalem at the center. If modern Americans and Europeans generally agree that north is the top and Europe is roughly the center, it is due primarily to a cartographic innovation by the sixteenth-century Flemish cartographer Gerardus Mercator. Because he conceived of a system of depicting longitude and latitude on a flat map of a round globe, sailors could use his maps to chart straight-line courses. For nearly four hundred years, this ingenious system was the world's most common projection for navigators' maps. Mercator-style maps loomed over a million classrooms in the United States for a century.

Mercator's map wasn't flawless, however. He vastly undercalculated the size of the earth, one of the technical flaws inherited from the existing authority, the Alexandrian astronomer and geographer Claudius Ptolemy, whose view of the world dated from more than a thousand years earlier. During the 1400s and well beyond Mercator, the error produced a global series of surprises and disappointments for explorers. The entire continent of North America and the vast Pacific Ocean are two prime examples. Mercator's grid system depended on incremental enlargements of the land areas moving away from the equator, which lies below the midpoint of his 1569 world map. On his projection, Europe's 3.8 million square miles look larger than South America's 6.9 million square miles, and Greenland looks larger than China (which is actually four times as large). He centered his projection on the country where he was born, Belgium, 50 degrees north of the equator. The exaggeration—which made what we now call first-world countries appear unrealistically large compared to some third-world countries—would, in the 1970s, generate charges of Eurocentrism by American academics. In fact, every projection must distort some aspect of the globe. Either the countries have the proper relative size (in which case the distances between them are wrong), or the distances are correct and the sizes are distorted. Since Mercator, hundreds of projections have been created, although relatively few are in anything like regular use.

Mercator's vision was criticized by the publishers of the controversial *Peters Atlas of the World*, who included a prefatory note: "The contents of the *Peters Atlas* are identical in all editions produced throughout the world." The note implies an editorial integrity that other atlases lack. But international maps are an international business, and what seems a simple and inspiring principle—one map for everyone—has never been realized. According to Juan José Valdés, assistant editor of maps for the National Geographic Society, the *Peters* note "is to assure the reader that the integrity of this atlas will not be altered by the rules and regulations set forth in the publication of maps and atlases by governments." However, he points out, map authorities in Ecuador will only recognize the pre-1942 Rio Protocol boundary delineation with Peru. The roots of the dispute concern the entire eastern frontier of Ecuador, known as the Oriente, scene of frequent invasions by Peru during the eighteenth and nineteenth centuries. Ecuador ceded a large part of the area to Peru in 1942, then renounced the cession in 1960. Today, Ecuadorian officials review all maps and atlases offered for sale in their country. "If the boundary with Peru is not properly delineated, the cartographic product cannot be sold or distributed," Valdés notes.

Dr. Michael Dobson, chief cartographer for Rand McNally Publishing Group, points out, "There are an awfully large number of small cartographic firms in the world that will put any name on a map that a customer wants." Or they'll leave off a troubling name. A huge wall mural of a world map made in Sweden for a Middle Eastern country doesn't show Israel. "Most world cartographers don't see anything wrong with leaving off a name if a client requests it," he says. Such pragmatism has long been a factor in world cartography. Consider the world map produced by Mateo Ricci, an Italian missionary who went to Guangdong province in China in 1583 to spread the gospel and gain support of the country's rulers. He accomplished the latter goal by studying the language and culture, eventually earning the trust of high officials, who allowed him in 1601 to enter Beijing, where he became a court mathematician and astronomer. The Chinese were intensely interested in Ricci's possessions, particularly his clocks and paintings, and eagerly studied his maps, which showed them modern Europe for the first time. He, in turn, sent back to Europe the first detailed reports of China. When, in 1602, he assembled what is now known as the Pekin map, he located the prime meridian 170 degrees east, which brought China into the middle. The position was anomalous in European maps, but it appealed to the Chinese.

I thought of Ricci's Pekin map when I visited a geography professor who had a new Chinese map of the world on the wall of his office. The projection showed China at dead center, with Europe and the Americas shoved out toward the edges. In Mandarin, China is Chug-hua Jen-min Kung-ho-kuo, the "central glorious people's united country." The name dates from 1000 B.C., when the people of the Chou dynasty on the North China Plain were unaware of the advanced civilizations in the West. They believed they occupied the middle of the earth, surrounded by barbarians. Visitors like Marco Polo and Mateo Ricci may have given the Chinese food for thought, but they didn't alter this basic perception.

The orientation of the continents is only one way that maps convey subtle agendas and reveal the ambitions of their makers. Some offer unvarnished propaganda, depicting disputed territory as belonging definitively to one country. Others, such as those made by the United Nations, work to reflect the international consensus. To understand a map, you must analyze both what it shows and what it doesn't show. According to Denis Wood, author of *The Power of Maps*, "We are always mapping the invisible or the unattainable or the erasable, the future or the past." Erasable because things do change, such as when the New Hebrides in the South Pacific, northeast of Australia, became Vanuatu. The new name celebrated the nation's independence, a final symbolic severing of any link with the original Hebrides, islands west of Scotland (Vanuatu's only connection to them was a visit by James Cook in 1774).

Prior to the nineteenth century, it was a rare map that didn't have its Terra Incognita or Debatable Land. However, "uninhabited" too often meant "except for aborigines." The notion of uninhabited lands set an attitudinal stage for colonization and largely accounted for the treatment of the indigenous inhabitants of the New World as savages. O. R. Dathorne writes in *Imagining the World*, "Clearly, if

DEREK NELSON

the continent were not habitable, then the people who lived there were nonpersons." In the sixteenth and seventeenth centuries, indigenous people were considered subhuman. European explorers divided the world into Christian and non-Christian peoples, the latter fair game for conquest and exploitation.

The motives of mapmakers were commercial more often than political. England and Portugal didn't sponsor two-year voyages into foreign seas as simple quests for knowledge; they were after trade, colonies, and raw materials. In many cases, a navigator's basic goal was to be able to get back to whatever marginally charted archipelago or green coast he had happened upon, and probably beyond it. Assuming he was making maps for his countrymen, he could assign any names he wanted, as long as they were distinctive, understandable, and not already in use. The Italian navigator Amerigo (Latinized to Americus) Vespucci, from whose name "America" is derived, could call Brazil "the Land of Saint Ambrose" (Tierra de S. Anbrosio) because, when his men rowed ashore, the aromas of the forest suggested a pun on the word "ambrosia."

The countries that produced the highest quality and quantity of maps were those whose fleets, by turns, dominated the seas: China, the Arab kingdoms, Greece, Italy, Portugal, the Netherlands, France, and Great Britain. These nations scattered a linguistic hodgepodge of place names around the globe; some stuck, and others (like the Land of Saint Ambrose) vanished.

In his youth, Portugal's Prince Henry the Navigator had listened spellbound to tales of African caravans trudging out of the Sahara laden with ivory, gold dust, and ostrich plumes. When he later had the power to dispatch explorers, his motives were not merely the acquisition of goods. He knew that expanded knowledge of geography would serve both his god and his king, and that trade would, of course, bring profit. Under succeeding rulers, the policies established by Prince Henry led to Portuguese navigator Bartholomeu Dias rounding the Cape of Good Hope in 1488 and opening the seaway to the Indies. By that time, King Manuel I was on Portugal's throne, and his sole focus was the Indies, the world's greatest source of wealth. He sent Vasco da Gama to find the way. In April 1498, da Gama found a rare ally at Malindi in present-day Kenya. The king, a Muslim, arranged for a Gujarati pilot, Ahmad ibn Majid, to guide the Portuguese explorers to India. The following month, da Gama anchored near Calicut, on the Malabar coast of India, and proceeded to destroy the established and peaceful system of Indian Ocean trade. Europeans began to wage nautical war on Eastern merchants and establish their own monopoly. Direct access effectively launched the Portuguese empire, which rapidly spanned the globe.

The name of da Gama's pilot has survived in the annals of world exploration, but other pilots who remain anonymous were crucial figures as well. Although captains' names fill history books and end up on maps (the Straits of Magellan was named after Ferdinand Magellan, who died before the remaining members of his 237-man crew completed the first successful navigation of the globe between 1519 and 1522), their accomplishments are also those of their chart makers. Is the name Pedro Reinel familiar? He was the foremost Portuguese cartographer of his time. After entering Spanish service, he settled in Seville, where he and his son made a globe and planisphere (a projection with an adjustable overlay that shows the stars visible at a particular time and place) for Magellan. How about the name Juan de la Cosa? He served as both pilot and chart maker for Columbus, later making three voyages to America on his own. The global success of the Dutch East India Company in the early 1600s was built on the efforts of mapmakers such as Petrus Plancius, one of dozens of official cartographers. The company's collection of 180 navigational maps, which showed such desperately competitive trade routes as the Indian archipelago, the route to India along Africa's coast, and the sea course to China, had the status of state secrets and, indeed, was called the Secret Atlas.

The military value of maps also contributed to their confidential status. During World War I, maps became increasingly precious and hard to acquire. When Assistant Secretary of the Navy Theodore Roosevelt ordered Asiatic Squadron Commander George Dewey to move American warships into Manila Bay, thereby launching the Spanish-American War, President William McKinley, who opposed the war, later admitted that he didn't know exactly where the Philippines were. In December 1941, President Franklin Roosevelt couldn't locate a small island near Borneo on any White House map. He dispatched an aide to the National Geographic Society's library, five blocks away. The island was found, and the society's map collection proved a prime resource for the duration of World War II. In the United States today, the Department of Defense's National Imagery and Mapping Agency is a critical source of federal cartographic expertise. Consistent names for obscure foreign locations are crucial to planners in headquarters, communicators who relay orders and situation reports and send troops into the field.

When the Polish city of Wrocław fell to Prussia in 1741, the invaders renamed it Breslau, which lasted until 1945, when it reverted to the original Polish version. Poland had savored several hundred years of autonomy before the

Prussian annexation, and the nation continued its fight for existence throughout the nineteenth and twentieth centuries. Germany invaded it during both world wars, and in each case Poland regained both its independence and Prussian territory, making the speedy and forceful rejection of German place-names inevitable.

The U.S. federal board charged with keeping track of such changes, the Board on Geographic Names, issued its First Report on Foreign Names in 1927 to record the myriad changes in boundaries and place-names that resulted from World War I. A prime example was the complex creation of Czechoslovakia, carved out of Austria (Bohemia, Moravia, and Silesia), Hungary (Slovakia and Carpathian Ruthenia), and Germany. Created in 1890, the board's first mandate was to standardize place-names in America's western territory. Reports of explorations, mining claims, and land surveys often referred to rivers, mountains, settlements, and other features by different names. Some names were new, others were taken from oral usage or respelled from French or Spanish documents. Today, the board reviews about one thousand new domestic names or suggested changes per year, approving less than a third.

The cartographer's problem of standardizing place-names is a given. Mapmakers inherit a variety of names from dozens of sources. Explorers sometimes recorded existing names (Cuba and Nicaragua, for example, were the names of native leaders), although the spelling was erratic and the pronunciation was invariably garbled. But invaders were more likely to impose new place names. Two dozen centuries of this activity produced the sort of atlas you'd expect to find in the Tower of Babel.

When a country publishes its own national atlas, it rarely encounters more than minor problems. But when countries try to cooperate on a multinational map, incompatible languages often snarl the process. Even if an English-speaking mapmaker decides to use Arabic forms of names, authorities disagree about how to spell those names in the Roman alphabet. Theoretically, diacritical marks can help readers sound out unusual foreign names, but since English doesn't employ any of these marks, many reference books omit them. The editors of one reference book point out that diacritical marks are "so numerous and so frequent in occurrence that their inclusion would serve to clutter the book, confuse the English-speaking reader, and raise serious problems in alphabetizing." In *World Facts and Figures*, each country has four kinds of names: conventional English-language, official, alternate, and former. Even after a country is renamed, divided, swallowed by another, or politically reorganized, its unofficial, popular name remains in use for decades. "Russia" was variously applied to the Russian Empire until 1917, then to both the Russian Soviet Federated Socialist Republic and the entire USSR until 1991, and finally to the entire modern Russian Federation since then.

Writing in his landmark 1909 study *Words and Places*, the Reverend Isaac Taylor cautioned: "Theorizing on the origin and meaning of a place-name in its modern form, without tracing its historical descent back to its oldest, and, if possible, primitive source, has over and over again proved a pitfall to engulf the light-hearted etymologer." Taylor wasn't much impressed with his predecessors and fellow scholars. Referring to a book published in London in 1773, he derided the author's "crude collection of ingenious conjectures and wild etymological dreams." He offered a humorous example, taken from a contemporary magazine. The word *Lambeth*, one might suppose (assuming just

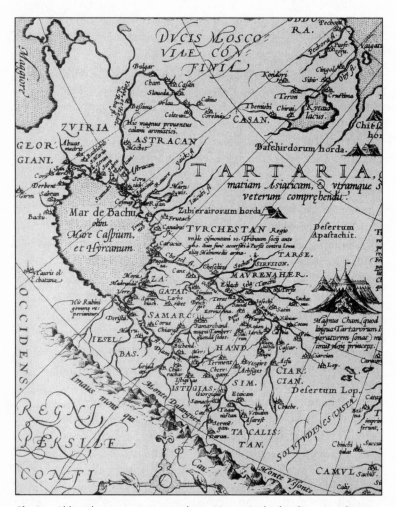

Fig. 2. *Although we are accustomed to seeing a single, familiar name for mountains, rivers, oceans, and countries, place-names usually exist in more than one version or language. These versions compete, clash, or coexist. Multiple names were a standard feature on medieval maps, recording native usage along with names assigned by later visitors or conquerors. In this 1570 view of Europe, the Caspian Sea has a trio of names. Mare Caspium refers to the Caspi tribe, who lived in the southern Caucasus, site of the first contacts with Romans and Greeks. Hyrcanum (written on other maps as Hircian and Hyrcanian) derived from another local tribe's name. The source of the third medieval name, Bachu, is a mystery. (Reproduced from the collections of the Library of Congress.)*

enough knowledge to be dangerous), derived from the Mongolian word *lama*, meaning "chief priest," and *beth*, Semitic for "house." Ergo, Lambeth must assuredly mean "house of the chief priest." The only problem was that it actually came from the Saxon *laom-hithe*, "muddy landing place." Taylor himself was posthumously forced to eat humble pie. In a later edition of his book, an editor added a note to one of the chapters, stating that some of his derivations had been disproved.

In 1995, news stories still placed Belgrade in "the former Yugoslavia," the federation of six republics (Serbia, Croatia, Bosnia and Herzegovina, Macedonia, Slovenia, and Montenegro) born of World War I. Some news maps still showed the place-name Yugoslavia, while others ceased using it. Montenegro and Serbia had reconstituted themselves as the Republic of Yugoslavia in April 1992, a new federation not recognized by the United Nations as possessing the status and rights of the old. Occasionally, the name was spelled Jugoslavia or Jugo-Slavia, a symbol, it seemed, both of an ideal of unity among this "Kingdom of the Serbs, Croats, and Slovenes," as it was originally proclaimed in 1918, and, inevitably, of its failure.

Not all place-names convey ominous messages, however. Some are straightforward: Ecuador is on the equator. Others are baffling: Greenland isn't very green. Still others startle or amuse, once you trace their hidden layers and complex linkages, reaching back through millennia. Place-names can also mark errors. The story goes that a British naval cartographer annotated a map of Alaska with the comment "Name?" above an unlabeled cape. A London printer apparently misread the query as "Nome" and so labeled it. (The name was later transferred to the nearby port, which had previously been called Anvil City.) The West Indies got their name because Columbus thought he was nearing southeast Asia. And still other sources are medieval myths, which echo in the names of the Amazon and Patagonia. Resurgent native names, such as Kalâtdlit Nunât for Greenland, reverse one highly visible result of colonialism. Place-names carry many meanings and implications, and in their curious histories, we can trace our own.

WHEN ETHNIC, CULTURAL, AND POLITICAL BOUNDARIES DON'T ALIGN

The classic case of a dysfunctional overlay of ethnic groups, geography, religions, and historic boundaries surrounds the state of Israel. In the 1890s, the Zionist movement began promoting a Jewish "national home." The League of Nations after World War I provided for the settlement to be in Palestine, then under British mandate. By 1920, 60,000 Jews lived in the area, along with ten times as many Arabs. The United Nations, which inherited oversight when Britain withdrew in 1948, approved a partition plan allowing for separate Jewish and Arab states.

Cartographers around the world began weighing de facto and de jure, redrawing boundaries, and selecting place-names. The new Israelites wanted a map that restored Hebrew place-names. Meron Benvenisti, a former deputy mayor of Jerusalem, recalls that the map was his father's lifework. Starting with British maps of Palestine from the 1880s, his father spent decades on research.

Jerusalem was envisioned as an internationally administered enclave in the projected Arab state. Fighting broke out even before a line could be drawn. Israel seized and designated as its capital the New City, which lies outside Jerusalem's four-quartered (Muslim, Jewish, Armenian, Christian) Old City; Transjordan took the Old City, annexed Samaria and Judaea (thereby erasing a couple of biblical names from the atlas), and renamed itself the Kingdom of Jordan. Most of the former Arab inhabitants of Israel became refugees in Gaza (a territory now held by Egypt), Jordan, and other Arab states. Sporadic wars ensued during the next thirty years. In the Six-Day War of 1967, Israel took the West Bank and Gaza (both with Arab populations), the Sinai to the Suez Canal, and the Golan Heights in Syria, bringing all of the original Palestine into Israeli hands. Cartographers grappled with this changing political geography. Hebrew names began to appear on maps of the West Bank, half of which, by 1986, was occupied by Israelis. That year there were 3.5 million Jews in Israel, 750,000 non-Jews (mostly Arabs) within the pre-1967 borders, and 1.25 million Jews in the West Bank and Gaza Strip.

To this day, Arab cartographers disregard Israel or call it Palestine. In Beirut, research institutes campaign for a Palestinian homeland by advancing a pre-1948 map of Palestine that does not show Jewish settlements, boundaries, or place-names. The left edge of a new Syrian tourist map runs through Beirut and the middle of the Dead Sea, which is unlabeled. Israel, not shown, lies somewhere off the map's edge. Other Syrian maps don't show Israel, either, reflecting a government policy aimed at denying the status quo. Syrian citizens openly discuss Israel, and television newscasts mention the country's name, but maps are another matter. Syrian maps also show part of the Golan as Syrian, as well as an area in the north called Iskenderun (which has been part of Turkey for fifty years).

A 1983 map entitled Arab World, published by GEO-projects of Beirut, Lebanon, and printed in Italy, includes a series of small paragraphs about the countries of the area, showing flags, land area, and languages. It includes an entry for Palestine, specifying that the area is "occupied" and that the population is "dispersed, mainly refugees." It lists the countries that border Palestine but doesn't mention Israel.

The editors of the 1985 edition of the *Times Atlas of the World* point out, "In recent years much political significance has been attached to the manner in which international boundaries are depicted and the way names are spelled in atlases." The editors stress that their goal is not to arbitrate territorial disputes but to show de facto boundaries at the time of publication.

For example, a 1970 Venezuelan map shows about three-fifths of Guyana as a "Zona en Reclamacion." The map uses a thick green border to mark national boundaries; the border around all of the area west of the Essequibo River is dotted, and tan stripes cover the zone. The roots of this dispute reach back to British claims over the old Dutch colonies of Essequibo, Demarara, and Berbice, which Great Britain acquired by treaty in 1814. Venezuela, after proclaiming its independence from Spain in 1811 and separating from the Great Columbia Union in 1830, inherited Spanish claims founded on settlements and missions established during the preceding three centuries. Venezuela and Guyana agreed to submit the boundary to arbitration in

1897, and a tribunal announced a decision in Paris two years later. In 1962, Venezuela declared that it had never recognized the decision. Today, Guyana possesses that huge territory, and prospects are dim that its neighbor will obtain it. Survey teams have mapped little of the dense rain forest covering the 400-mile border, a fact hindering solutions to the dispute.

The 1975 edition of the *Hammond International World Atlas* prints the following disclaimer on a map of the USSR: "The government of the United States has not recognized the incorporation of Estonia, Latvia and Lithuania into the Soviet Union, nor does it recognize as final the de facto western limit of Polish administration in Germany (the Oder-Neisse line)." Versions of the disclaimer appeared on American maps for decades after World War II. Estonia, Latvia, and Lithuania all border Russia on the east and were nominally independent in 1918. Overrun by the German army at the outset of World War II, they were annexed by the USSR in August 1940. The Oder-Neisse line was the Poland-Germany boundary established in 1945 by the Potsdam Conference, which gave additional land to Poland in partial compensation for some Polish territories annexed by the USSR. Poland solidified its claim by expelling German inhabitants of the region. The former East Germany recognized the line in 1950, as did West Germany in 1971. The dissolution of the USSR obviated the first part of the disclaimer.

War is the most prolific creator of misalignments between boundaries and ethnic groups. After the 1917 revolution in Russia, the Turki peoples in Central Asia fought to regain their independence. When the new Soviet government suppressed their revolts, a million Kazaks fled across the Chinese border, and millions of Russians settled in Kazakstan, where they now greatly outnumber the original inhabitants. After World War II, millions of Chinese were settled in Xinjiang (which had been peopled by Uighurs and Kazaks) and in Inner Mongolia. In both regions, Chinese now outnumber the original inhabitants.

The same thing happened in Tibet, which first came under Chinese control in 1720, during the Manchu dynasty. Communist Chinese invaded the country in the early 1950s, and large numbers of Chinese settled there, eventually outnumbering the Tibetans. By early 1995, the population of the capital city of Lhasa was at least 50 percent non-Tibetan. The Chinese government refers to Tibet as an "autonomous region," but Beijing controls the region's religion, economy, and politics.

Whether forced out by a central government or driven away by warfare, migrating peoples invariably threaten political maps. When France began to withdraw from Vietnam, it first left the north, and 800,000 Vietnamese fled south, sketching a political dividing line that would later materialize on maps during the Vietnam War. An estimated 5 million refugees were adrift throughout Africa by the mid-1980s, scattered by postcolonial events such as the annexation of Somaliland by Somalia (a country in east Africa on the Indian Ocean), which became independent in 1960. This action triggered a series of border clashes, resulting from the nationalist aims of Muslim Somalis living in eastern Kenya, in the Ogaden and Haud regions in southeastern Ethiopia, and in Djibouti (in east Africa on the Gulf of Aden at the entrance to the Red Sea).

Old geographic problems have also collided in modern Macedonia, whose name, as late as 1996, had to be written with quotation marks or, as it appeared in the roster of the United Nations, as the former Yugoslav Republic of Macedonia. Ancient Macedonia included parts of modern Greece and Bulgaria. Its history is particularly complex and turbulent. From its roots as a Greek-speaking area in the eighth century B.C., Macedon became the first Roman province in the second century B.C., was conquered in succession by the Byzantine Empire, the Slavs, and Bulgaria in the ninth century, then by the Byzantines again, the Serbs, and finally the Ottoman Turks, who held it for more than five hundred years. In the late nineteenth century, powerful terrorist organizations supported by Bulgaria began pushing for Macedonian independence. Regional wars in the early twentieth century divided Macedonia among Greece, Serbia, and Bulgaria.

Since 1926, Bulgaria has pressed the greatest territorial claim to parts of Macedonia, on the tenuous basis of a brief union that dissolved with the death of Alexander the Great. Bulgaria refuses to acknowledge the Macedonian ethnic group—Slav Macedonians, as they are often called to distinguish them from Greek Macedonians, who inhabit the Greek province Macedonia—as being distinct from the Bulgarian one. Admittedly, the question is long-standing. Writing in *National Geographic* in 1923, the linguist A. L. Guerard asked, "Is Macedonia by blood preponderantly Greek, Bulgarian, or Serbian? This question, submerged, but not settled, by the Turkish conquest, for 500 years has formed a central problem of the Near East."

Macedonia lacks international recognition because the Greek government disputes the country's use of the name Macedonia. Greeks assert that Macedon was historically part of Greece and anticipate future territorial disputes if the name is formally revived as an independent nation. Yet the country exports products labeled "Made in Macedonia."

Linguistic differences can also play a role in solidifying and magnifying existing conflicts between ethnic groups. Voluntary immigrants to a new country often want to assimilate, but when a group of people who share traditions, culture, organizations, language, and religion are subsumed by a larger state, assimilation is anathema. Such groups are nearly ineradicable, even if they lack a homeland and a political system. The Kurds in eastern Turkey, linked to a terrorist movement called the PKK (Kurdish Workers Party), have produced a local state of emergency for twenty years. With ethnic kin in the former Soviet Union and throughout the Caucasus, they aspire to a state called Kurdistan, a place created by the Treaty of Sèvres in 1920 between the Allies (except Russia and the United States) and the Ottoman Empire when the latter was liquidated. Turkey retained Anatolia (Asia Minor) and was charged, under the terms of the treaty, to grant autonomy to Kurdistan. The plan failed when Kemal Atatürk's nationalists overthrew the former sultan, whose government had accepted the treaty. The Treaty of Lausanne (1922–23) reversed some elements of the Treaty of Sèvres. Turkey retained sovereignty over all of its territory; the new treaty did not mention the establishment of a Kurd nation.

Wales has been a principality of England since 1536, but it has nevertheless maintained a distinctive Welsh culture and has fought to keep its language, called Cymric, alive. Twenty percent of the population still speak Cymric; two hundred years ago, half the population did. Although a referendum on Welsh independence failed in 1979, some nationalist agitation continues, focused on the right to be educated in Welsh. In the early 1960s, nationalists founded Cymdeithas yr Iaith Gymraeg (the Welsh Language Society), using civil disobedience and public protest to obtain such visible concessions as Cymric road signs, which show the town of Cardigan as Aberteifi, and Holyhead as Caergybi. The Cymric name for Britain, incidentally, is Prydain.

Map boundaries and language differences were key to longtime problems in the former provinces of Trento and Bolzano on the northern border of Italy. A German-speaking majority lives in Bolzano, an area that was part of Austria (the South Tirol, or Südtirol) before 1918. When it was transferred to Italy after World War I, the Italians renamed it Venezia Tridentina, and the fascist government enforced Italian as the official language. In the late 1940s, a new republican constitution allowed German speakers to set up schools, but in the 1950s, Bolzano was joined with the province of Trento to form a region called Trentino-Alto Aldige, which had an Italian-speaking majority. This merger caused serious friction between Italy and Austria, ultimately bringing several issues before the World Court for solution. In 1972, the region was given increased legislative and administrative autonomy.

Language problems may foreshadow changes in maps and place-names in Sri Lanka, the former Ceylon, a tear-drop-shaped tropical island in the Indian Ocean, where the ethnic makeup is 69 percent Sinhalese (Theravada Buddhists) and 25 percent Hindu Tamil. Ancestors of the Tamil have lived on the island for a thousand years. In 1956, the government tried to mandate the use of Sinhala, and Tamil rioters responded with demands for official recognition of the Tamil language and establishment of a separate state, Tamil Eelam. Battling toward that end in 1986, Tamil guerrillas seized an area in the dense jungles of the far north around Jaffna. Simultaneously, a radical Sinhalese student force, protesting the insufficiently punitive treatment of the guerrillas, ambushed and sometimes assassinated government figures. The government summoned Indian troops the following year, which fought the guerrillas rather unsuccessfully, withdrawing in 1989. By the mid-1990s, tens of thousands had died.

In Canada a near majority in Quebec, while satisfied with their place-name, demand independence and threaten secession. Canada was settled by French explorers in the sixteenth and seventeenth centuries, and French Canadians retained political and religious rights after Britain acquired Quebec in 1763. The confederation of Canada was formed in 1867. Demands for treatment as an equal partner and recognition of Quebec's "unique" culture forced the Canadian government to restore the status of the French language in the 1960s. As a result, Canada now has two official languages, although Quebec is the only province with a French-speaking majority. It is Canada's largest province, slightly larger than France, and has 25 percent of the country's population, of whom more than nine out of ten speak French. However, fewer than 10 percent of the people in Ontario, which is the second largest province, speak French. English-speaking Canadians object to spending federal money on bilingual forms and magazines. In Quebec, meanwhile, the city government ignores the bilingual mandate and erects signs in French only. Before Canada's 1995 vote on secession, Prime Minister Jean Chretien went on national television to ask, "Are you really ready to tell the whole world that people of different languages, different backgrounds, different cultures, cannot live together?" Secession was averted by a margin of just 1 percent, 50.5 percent to 49.5 percent.

With varying degrees of success, government planners often work to overcome linguistic and ethnic conflicts by redrawing internal maps. Belgium's two ethnic and cultural regions, Flanders and Wallony, continually strike sparks; part of the problem has been linguistic. Flemings, in the north, are descendants of Germanic Franks and speak a language that is a variant of Dutch. In the south, the Walloons, descended from Celts, speak French, though a small, largely elderly segment of the population also speak Walloon (a Romance language with some German influence). In the early 1900s, when 60 percent of the Belgian people spoke Flemish, French was the official language of the government, the military, and many newspapers. Because France had repeatedly posed threats to Belgium's independence in the past, Flemings felt justified in their hostility to the dominance of the French language. During the 1960s and 1970s, independent Flemish and Walloon assemblies were created, and Flemish was decreed an official state language. The name Flanders appears in modern atlases; Wallony does not.

In some places, intranational autonomy appears to have provided longer-lasting solutions. Switzerland, with its German-speaking majority and Italian and French minorities, has perhaps the least centralized power of any developed nation. Shortly after World War II, the French-speaking Jura district, which had included (since 1815) the German-speaking canton of Berne, spawned Catholic and Protestant Jurassian separatist parties, leading it to become the twenty-third canton.

The definition of "autonomy" is elastic, however. True autonomy implies control of social and political policies, and some central governments prove autocratic. The late, unlamented Soviet Union on paper identified itself as a federation of fifteen republics. The largest of the republics was Russia, containing another sixteen smaller autonomous republics made up of various nationalities (such as Buryat Mongolian, Tatar, and Yakut). The "Big Three" conference attended by Roosevelt, Churchill, and Stalin at Yalta in 1945 provided that the liberated people of Europe would be able to "create democratic institutions of their own choice," a proviso the USSR ignored.

The Soviet government, instead, created a nightmare place that didn't appear on maps: the Gulag Archipelago, in Aleksandr Solzhenitsyn's haunting phrase. "Gulag" is a Russian acronym for the government department in charge of labor camps. The network of more than two thousand prison camps once had an estimated population of 10 million; several million prisoners died. Speaking out for freedom or autonomy, whether personal, local, or regional, was one way to earn a visit.

Banishing people to the gulag didn't dissolve ethnic tensions. During the mid-1980s, the rapid rate of population growth among some of the central Asian peoples, including Uzbeks and Kazakhs, worried the central powers in Moscow, who rightly perceived it as a source of nationalist sentiment. Long-term, formal repression failed to eradicate similar feelings in the Baltic republics, in Armenia, Georgia, and Azerbaijan in the Caucasus, and in Ukraine. One-sixth of the population of the USSR was Muslim; at existing growth rates, that ratio might have reached one-quarter by the year 2000, a factor that would have certainly added pressure to the Soviet system had it not collapsed.

Picture the members of the League of Nations after World War I, crawling around on a huge map of the world spread out on the floor of an office in Paris, drawing partitions and spheres of influence and territories. The map depicted a European consensus view of national borders. Part of its creation was the former Yugoslavia. Today, other nations are trying to accomplish a similar feat in the same place, working with an international proposal that, at one stage, recommended that 51 percent of Bosnia be a Muslim-Croat federation and 49 percent be Serbian. In his column on September 8, 1995, George Will likened the effort to unscrambling eggs. A major problem, Will observed, was that "each side's cartographic version of 51-49 looks awfully like 60-40 in their favor."

Sixty-three percent of all national conflicts between 1945 and 1968 flared between bordering nations. At least one hundred officially recognized boundary disputes simmer in the world at any given time. Perhaps because empires are no longer there to keep them in place, the redrawing of boundaries no longer seems an effective way to resolve conflict. Before World War II, Silesia and Pomerania were located southwest of Poland, between Germany and Czechoslovakia. During the eighteenth and nineteenth centuries, the upper and middle classes in Silesia were mostly German, and the workers mostly Polish. The Treaty of Versailles in 1919 provided a plebiscite in Silesia to determine whether the region would be German or Polish. Results favored Germany except in the industrial region of eastern Upper Silesia, where Poles predominated. The League of Nations partitioned the territory, with most of the industrial district passed to the new nation of Poland. To further complicate matters, the district of Teschen was later partitioned between Poland and Czechoslovakia. Boundaries were drawn so arbitrarily that they ran right through the middle of mines, leaving some workers with a job in one country and a home in another. Nazi Germany held Silesia during World War II until the Red Army attacked in 1945. With the Potsdam Conference, Poland reclaimed most of the territory. A subsequent massive migration of Germans from Silesia left a Polish majority, assuring final Polish sovereignty.

The misalignment of political boundaries and ethnic groups sometimes generates provisional place-names on the world map. The history of Cyprus is one such example. First colonized by Greeks and Phoenicians, Cyprus was under Turkish rule for more than three centuries, starting in

1570. Great Britain then acquired it, ruling until 1960. The postindependence constitution gave a share of power to the Turkish minority (four-fifths of Cyprus's half-million citizens were Greek). Fourteen years later, the military government ruling Greece staged a military coup in Nicosia, the capital of the Mediterranean island, with the aim of reuniting Cyprus and Greece. A Turkish invasion in 1974 divided the island between Greece and Turkey, and nine years later, territorial leaders declared the establishment of the Turkish Republic of Northern Cyprus, which only Turkey recognizes as sovereign. Today, a buffer zone, known as the Green Line, is patrolled by the United Nations.

India has generated perhaps the most violent and convoluted geographic problems of any modern nation. Its Muslim minority campaigned for a separate state during the 1940s. At the same time, proponents of independence from Great Britain who came to be known as "freedom fighters," under Mohandas K. Gandhi, ended an epic struggle notable for mass, widespread adherence to the principle of civil disobedience. Achievement of independence was by no means entirely peaceful, of course. In 1946, Indian Navy personnel mutinied aboard ships, one of the movement's final violent incidents. "Midnight hour," as Jawaharlal Nehru, India's first prime minister, called the moment when power was transferred from Britain to India, marked the birth of the republic on August 15, 1947. Partition of India, by the last British governor-general, Lord Louis Mountbatten, created Pakistan, its West and East sections separated by a thousand miles of India. The hoped-for peaceful coexistence of this predominantly Muslim nation and India, which is predominantly Hindu, did not materialize through partition; instead, it intensified religious divisiveness. The conflict escalated to war, and hundreds of thousands of Muslims and Hindus uprooted themselves.

Divided Pakistan, whose Punjab province had itself been divided to allow India access to the mountain provinces of Kashmir and Jammu, went to war with India in 1947. Although a 1949 UN cease-fire ended the conflict, it erupted again in 1965.

The Indo-Pakistan war of that year left Pakistan in control of a northwestern territory called Azad Kashmir, with India holding the rest, but this status is "in dispute," according to a current U.S. State Department map showing the 1965 cease-fire line. Other maps produced in the United States cite Kashmir and Jammu as being "claimed by both Pakistan and India." Other American and British atlases show areas occupied by each country and claimed by the other; four places occupied by China and claimed by India, Pakistan, or both; and an area that India occupies but that China claims. Maps from all three countries portray geographic optimism. A Chinese map shows both the disputed boundary between Pakistan and India with the legend "Area actually controlled by . . ." on each side and, as undisputed Chinese territory, an area east of the Karakorum Mountains claimed by India. American publishers discovered that they couldn't export books containing identical maps of Jammu and Kashmir to China and India, because each country demanded a different version.

Arguably the most definitive map change in the region occurred on March 16, 1971, with the declaration of independence by East Pakistan as the new republic of Bangladesh. Mounting Bengali demands for greater self-government in East Pakistan—in particular, the right to speak Bengali instead of Urdu—had met with repressive government action that led to civil war. India entered the conflict, the day after independence on the side of Bangladesh, formally recognizing the republic.

In 1988, newspapers in the Philippines reported that

Malaysia had annexed the Turtle Islands, which lie just off the coast of the Sabah state in northern Malaysia and are part of the Tawitawi province of the Philippines. For several days, maps depicted the alleged Malaysian encroachment. The incident, however, proved to be a false alarm, a Philippine naval officer's misinterpretation of a line on an American navigation chart that marked the recommended route for tankers and freighters passing the Turtle Islands, which he took to be the recently defined boundary of Malaysia's exclusive economic zone. The officer's error was understandable: maps don't just depict facts, they send ominous messages and trace ethnic and religious fault lines that can change the map itself.

THE WAR BETWEEN DISTORTION AND ACCURACY

"THE ANTS ALONG THE NIGER WERE AS BIG AS MASTIFFS"

With serpents cruising distant seas and dog-headed people prowling faraway lands, antique maps resembled latter-day tabloids. But tabloids merely entertain, while the varieties of distortion on old maps, and the reasons behind them, are multifarious. Copyists made errors. Translators garbled text. Cartographers—the profession was made up largely of artists in other fields, who at first simply copied old maps and embellished them with decoration—relied on navigators who made their charts using mediocre instruments and crude navigational techniques. Information blended with a peculiar combination of folklore, religion, and instruction. Christian monks and Islamic mullahs added allegory. All these ingredients helped produce extraordinary maps, full of color and lively detail—entertaining, but useless for planning an itinerary.

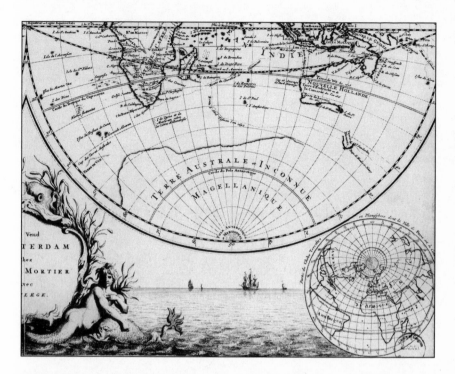

Fig. 3. Note the incomplete coastlines drawn in the South Pacific on this map from 1700. Where earlier mapmakers filled in the blanks with wild guesses, the increase of geographic knowledge made serious cartographers more aware of the limits of their information; the resulting maps were less entertaining, but more credible. (Reproduced from the collections of the Library of Congress.)

In cartographic history, knowledge did not increase steadily; progress was more like two steps forward, three steps back, and several off in random directions. Milestones were followed by serious regressions. The Phoenicians, a seafaring Semitic people from the Syrian-Lebanese coast, sailed the Mediterranean, to Cyprus, North Africa, France, Spain, and on into the Atlantic, to the west coast of Africa, and perhaps as far as Britain. They were so skillful and renowned that, between 700 B.C. and 500 B.C., the Egyptian pharaoh Necho reportedly commissioned a Phoenician admiral to sail around Africa. Accounts say he dispatched ships south from the Red Sea. It took three years to round the continent and eventually reach Egypt. Two thousand years later, the Portuguese navigator Bartholomeu Dias had to feel his way in the dark along these same coasts.

Two hundred years before the birth of Christ, the Greek astronomer Eratosthenes calculated a circumference of the earth that was about 15 percent too large (he clearly perceived the world was round, as did Ptolemy). Yet in medieval Europe, just before the Age of Discovery, the best guess of the world's size was more than a quarter too small, and many Christians rejected the notion that the earth was spherical.

During the second and third centuries B.C., Alexandria was the Roman capital of Egypt under the Ptolemies, the dynasty of fourteen kings who ruled from 300 B.C. until 30 B.C. Alexandria became the hub of commerce and the greatest city of the Hellenic world, its library drawing astronomers, mathematicians, doctors, historians, and philosophers from everywhere. For four centuries, the city endured as the intellectual center of the empire. In the second century A.D., Ptolemy was its foremost scholar. He wrote an extensive text about the theory and practice of cartography, described how to calculate geographic coordinates using meridians and parallels, and compiled a massive gazetteer.

Although Ptolemy synthesized a great deal of valuable and accurate information and greatly advanced the theoretical knowledge of geography, his depiction of the world was riddled with misconceptions. He underestimated the size of the earth, which, incidentally, he placed at the center of the universe. Europe and Asia covered more than half the world, drastically shrinking the western ocean that presumably separated Europe and Asia. When Ptolemy's theories were revived in medieval Europe, the error encouraged explorers to challenge the mysterious seas to the west. Ptolemy showed southern Africa connected to Asia, which would derail the European search for a sea route to the Indies for centuries.

With the gradual destruction of the Alexandrian library following the invasion of Julius Caesar's armies in 30 B.C., Ptolemy's work was lost to the West until the fourteenth century. Fortunately, traveling scholars had shared the cartographic trove with Arab countries, so the growth of geographic knowledge was merely relocated, not halted.

Furthermore, although China was unknown to Ptolemy, ancient cartographers had mapped that kingdom before 1100 B.C. After the invention of paper in the second century B.C., the Chinese government formed a department responsible solely for mapmaking. At about the time Ptolemy was at work in Alexandria, a Chinese cartographer, Pei Hsiu, compiled an official government manual on mapmaking. The result was a series of sophisticated, accurate, and detailed maps of the regions of China. During the expansionist T'ang dynasty from 618 to 907, a sixty-volume collection of geographic descriptions and maps of the lands in the West was assembled, of which only descriptions survive. The dynasty, founded with the aid of Turkish allies, was open to foreign ideas and traded with Korea, Japan, and Vietnam. Chinese cartography reached another peak between the twelfth and fifteenth centuries, when Chinese navigators and merchants launched great expeditions to southeast Asia, India, the Persian Gulf, and eastern Africa, looking for tribute and trade. The ships were equipped with the most accurate and informative maps yet developed.

The rulers of the Abbasid court in Iraq, circa 750–775, recruited Hindu geographers for strategic purposes. The first references to Arab maps date from the eighth century;

they were used for planning sieges and analyzing combat. Al-Ma'mun, a caliph, assembled a "world map" in the early 800s, but, like similar maps of early rulers, it showed only his territories. The earliest set of surviving Islamic maps was from a group of cartographers known as the Balkhi School, circa 900. Geometric and stylized views of the empire's territories, they mainly showed caravan routes and lacked scale, latitude, and longitude.

As the Dark Ages descended upon Europe, the Byzantine lands appropriated the scientific and practical knowledge of classical Greece and Rome. Beginning in the eighth century, Muslim scholars had access to the works of Greek scientists stored in libraries in Constantinople and other centers of the Byzantine Empire. In the ninth and tenth centuries in Baghdad, a massive program of translating Greek science into Arabic began; the effort was central to the flowering of Arab culture through the thirteenth century. Ptolemy's writings formed the basis of Islamic astronomy and astrology. Traces of his geography appear, for instance, in the work of the cartographer al-Khwarazmi, who in 850 produced a map of the Nile that showed the Mountains of the Moon, which Ptolemy seems to have considered the river's source. British expeditions even set out to find these mountains as late as the nineteenth century.

Ptolemy's legacy conveyed various fallacies to Arab mapmakers, who, from the seventh through the twelfth centuries, generally believed that the Indian Ocean was a land-locked southern sea. Although they accepted the idea that the world was spherical, they had difficulty conceiving of the other hemisphere and decided it must be uninhabitable. Arab navigators gradually disproved some of Ptolemy's theories, but it was to their advantage to foster the belief that the only pass to the riches of the East lay over

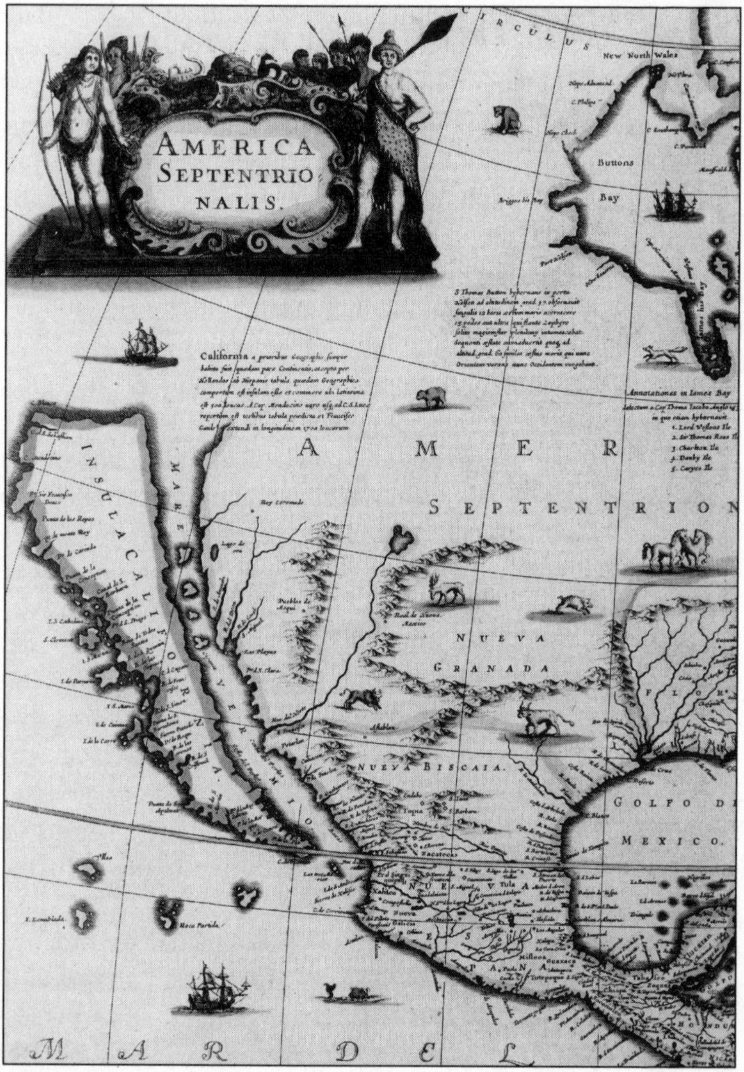

Figs. 4 and 5. These two maps illustrate the ebb and flow of geographic knowledge. The 1639 map showing California as an island represents a curious regression, because earlier maps (such as the adjoining one from 1570) accurately showed it as a peninsula. Note the close proximity of Japan. The vast Pacific was far from getting its due, and Europeans were still hoping that the riches of the Orient were a short sail away. (Reproduced from the collections of the Library of Congress.)

DEREK NELSON

land, where they controlled the caravan routes. Thus medieval Arab scholars continued to describe the Atlantic as boundless, "the Green Sea of Darkness." To the south lay a gigantic country that was too hot to support life.

Other Arab mapmakers were more concerned with the

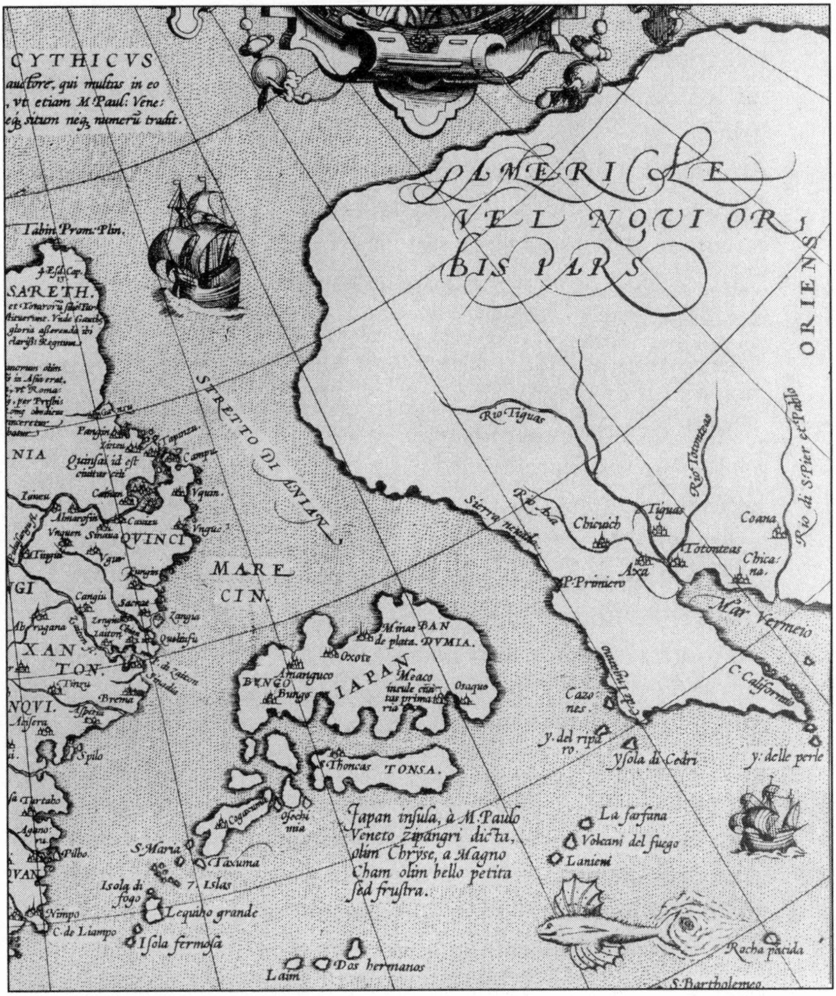

heavens than with the earth. Inspired by a passage from the Qur'an ("It is He who has appointed for you the stars, that you might be guided by them in the darkness of the land and sea"), they developed an intricate celestial cartography, symbolic and allegorical, depicting the supernatural and the natural. Such maps had an extensive tradition in the East among Buddhist, Jain, and Hindu philosophers and scholars. Maps drawn between 700 and 800 show constellations of the zodiac. Ancient versions of the zodiac intertwined with systems of moon and sun worship and with beliefs that stars and planets influenced human affairs. Arab astronomers christened many stars familiar to English speakers. Ceti, near the constellation Pisces, was *al-qitus*, originally a sea monster but later identified as a whale. Persei (also known as Algol) in the constellation Perseus was *al-ghul*, "the ghoul." Betelgeuse derives from *bayt al-jawza*, "the house of the twins." The texts from Ptolemy included a catalog of 1,025 stars, which became the basis of Arabic celestial globes.

Realistic cartography flourished in Islamic Spain, in the southern region the Arabs named al-Andalus, during the tenth and eleventh centuries. Cordoba was then a city of a half-million people, a center of scientific scholarship (particularly mathematics and astronomy), technology, and philosophy. Geography, in part because of its links with economics and politics, was another primary field of research. As-Sharif al-Idrisi, perhaps the most famous medieval geographer and cartographer, was educated there in the early 1100s. Although he was from a family of caliphs from Ceuta in Morocco, he joined the court of the Norman King Roger II at Palermo. Roger planned to conquer Islamic Spain and the western Mediterranean. Al-Idrisi directed fifteen years of research aimed at producing accurate and reliable maps to guide these conquests, thereby providing the only direct connection between Arab and European geography. His approach was to divide the known world into seventy sections, with extensive descriptions of the physical, cultural, and social aspects of each place.

Cartography in medieval Europe, as we have seen, was considerably less accurate. Apart from lacking a solid foundation in science, many cartographers turned their attention from the natural to the supernatural. Mountain-sized fish, werewolves, dog-headed apes, and other bizarre creatures became staples. Modern scholars trace them mainly to the third century Roman compiler Gaius Julius Solinus, who reached deep into a thirty-seven-volume encyclopedia of natural science written by Pliny the Elder (A.D. 23–79), a Roman naturalist. Although much of Pliny's science was secondhand, ironically, he died collecting firsthand data (he was asphyxiated investigating the eruption at Vesuvius). Solinus produced one of the most popular books of the Middle Ages: an encyclopedia of wondrous tales called *Collectanea rerum memorabilium*, which endured through the sixteenth century.

In Asia, Solinus located Gryphons, a fierce species of fowl that could tear people to bits. In Germany, he described birds whose feathers glowed in the dark. Near the Niger River in West Africa, ants grew to the size of large dogs. These and dozens of other chimera were the precursors of map illustrations such as one drawn in 1367, showing the mythical island of Mayda with a trio of Breton ships in the vicinity. One of the ships is half-sunken, grasped in the tentacles of an octopus-like sea monster. Overhead, an airborne dragon gnaws a human dinner. North of Labrador was a terrible place called the Isles of Demons. The isles first appeared, embellished with drawings of fiendish imps and labeled "Insulae Demonium," on a 1507 map made by Johann Ruysch, notable because his world map was the first to show any part of the New World.

Western maps after Ptolemy became more ecclesiastic than cartographic, as mapmakers drew them to meet biblical specifications. A scriptural reference to "the four corners of the earth" meant the world must be rectangular. Paradise had to be in the east (usually at the top of the map). A map of England made by a Benedictine monk in 1250 distorts the shape of the country in order to accentuate the route from Doncaster to Dover, where pilgrims embarked to Rome. The most famous medieval world map dates from about 1300 and resides in England's Hereford Cathedral. Its center is Jerusalem, and it includes a drawing of Noah's ark. Empty spaces are crammed with drawings from popular histories and bestiaries.

Just as the transcribed narrations of early Arabic literature were a mix of *akhbar* (historical narratives) and *'aja'ib* (stories about marvelous events and things), maps became an amalgam of truth and fiction. In the mid-1400s, an Italian monk-cartographer, Fra Mauro from Murano, near Venice, included on a world map he was preparing for the king of Portugal a textual note about a ship from India blown off course for forty days. The ship, he wrote, encountered a fabulous bird called a roc, which had a wingspan of sixty paces and could carry an elephant in its talons. The creature had somehow escaped from the tales of *Arabian Nights*, dated five hundred years earlier.

Among the more durable legends was a place known as the Islands of Saint Brendan, named after an Irish abbot from County Galway who was born in 484 and died in 578. This abbot apparently undertook a voyage to verify the existence of a paradisical island. He found such a place, which he later described in a hyperbole-filled account, where the souls of blessed mortals went to live on after death. The legend dovetailed with a couple of much older myths: the old Greek and Roman belief in the Hesperides (where daughters of Atlas guarded a wondrous garden containing golden apples, located at the western extremity of the world) and the old Celtic belief in a paradise called Avalon in the western sea. The place came to be noted on maps as the "Blessed Isles," with Brendan the protagonist in the Irish version, though similar legends could also be found in Latin, English, French, Saxon, Flemish, Welsh, Breton, and Scottish Gaelic cultures.

The islands first appeared on the Hereford map mentioned earlier. Other medieval maps showed Saint Brendan's discovery vaguely northwest of Africa, labeled "Fortunate Insulae sex sunt Sct Brandani" (the Six Fortunate Islands of Saint Brendan). Sometimes the islands were identified with the Madeiras or Azores; more often they meandered around the ocean. They appeared on maps and globes until the mid-1700s, often with a robust Brendan in what became a standard pose, astride a sea serpent.

The legendary Prester John was equally ubiquitous on medieval maps ("prester" means priest or presbyter). Said to rule a kingdom encompassing Africa, Asia, or both—depending on the source of the legend—his saga, according to some accounts, started in 1122, when a priest named Giovanni arrived in Rome at the invitation of Pope Calixtus II. Giovanni announced that he had come from the capital city of a powerful sect of Indian Christians. He vividly described the wealth of India and the strength of its Christians, who were headed by a priest named John and whose existence seemed a promising chink in the heathen armor. Although his story clearly placed the priest in India, some early maps showed him in Europe. A 1490 world map showed a country labeled "India Orientalis" and noted that

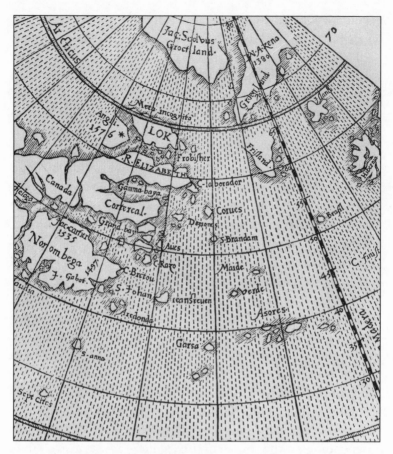

ABOVE: **Fig. 6.** Two mythical islands appear on this 1582 map by British cartographer Michael Lok. The long-sought island of Saint Brendan was supposedly an Edenic place where the souls of humans lived after death; this island appears at center, north of the quite real Azores. To the right is an imaginary island called Brasil. Although this island later vanished from maps, the name found a new home in South America. (Reproduced from the collections of the Library of Congress.)

RIGHT: **Fig. 7.** Some imaginary places simply disappeared from maps; others gradually merged with real places. Here, the Hesperides (where, according to Greek myth, the daughters of Atlas guarded a tree bearing golden apples) are identified with the Cape Verde Islands. (Reproduced from the collections of the Library of Congress.)

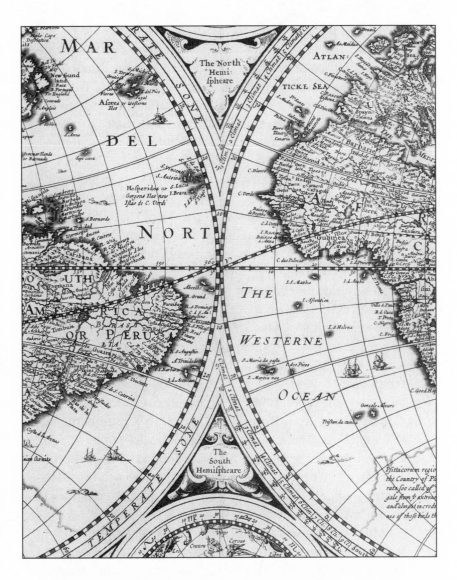

it included the realm of Prester John, "emperor of all India." The myth accreted detail over time, with one version claiming that Prester John commanded seventy-two vassal kings.

Among the adherents to the myth was Prince Henry of Portugal. Henry was the third son of John I and would have remained an obscure prince had he not decided to test the belief that the waters of the equator were boiling. He became famous as "the Navigator," and his conquest of Ceuta in the early fifteenth century was the first European foothold in Africa since the days of Roman conquest. Henry was fascinated by Africa; it was in Ceuta that he first heard of Prester John. As Henry pushed his nation's exploration of the African coast, one of his primary goals was to find the rich and powerful priest and join forces with his Christian army to outflank and defeat the Muslim countries on the Mediterranean, with a triumphant march on to Jerusalem and eternal glory. Portuguese explorers did manage to go around the continent, but the glory they found was commercial, not spiritual.

In the interior of Africa, Prester John continued to elude discovery. In 1455, reports placed his kingdom just six days' journey from Gambia. In a map published by Abraham Ortelius (who, along with Mercator, developed the modern atlas), Prester John's kingdom encompasses eastern and central Africa, from Egypt in the north to Mozambique in the south. A 1558 atlas by Portuguese cartographer Diogo Homem shows a resplendent Prester John straddling northeast Africa. Three palace turrets loom behind him. He wears a golden cloak, red sandals, and a large crown and sits on a huge throne.

Although these and other myths would haunt maps for another two hundred years, a steadily increasing flow of precise data was beginning to arrive from distant lands. During the Renaissance, Marco Polo's accounts of thirteenth-century Persia, Japan, Sumatra, the Andaman Islands, and eastern Africa to Zanzibar served as one of the few sources of information on the East, but not until the late 1800s would Europeans gather accurate material on much of central Asia. Polo's naming of three nonexistent lands—Beach, Luchach, and Maletur—in the vicinity of Australia did not detract from his credibility.

Barcelona became another center of cartographic knowledge in the thirteenth and fourteenth centuries, due in part to an influx of Jewish scholars escaping the wars between the Berber Almoravid and Almohad sects in Morocco and Spain, and Berber persecution elsewhere in north Africa. These scholars brought Arab learning about geography and astronomy. Led by Abraham Cresques, cartographer for King Peter III of Aragon, they made the first serious European effort to include Asia, the Orient, and the western oceans in European world maps. Existing maps, portolans, and the narratives of thirteenth- and fourteenth-century travelers helped produce a masterpiece: the Catalan atlas, the earliest medieval map that approximated Asia's true shape. Of particular note was the complete absence of speculation. The effort banished many medieval fables from Spanish maps. Cresques's son later served Prince Henry of Portugal as a teacher of cosmography and chart making.

The transition from medieval to Renaissance cartography is also apparent in the work of Fra Mauro. His world map was circular, more than six feet in diameter, drawn on parchment, and mounted on wood. He abandoned the convention of centering maps on Jerusalem and successfully sought firsthand sources of information, among them charts of the latest discoveries, provided by the Portuguese king. Japan appears for the first time on a European map, shown as Zimpangu. In Burma, he showed the city of Perhe written in the authentic Burmese form. He noted that he got details of his depiction of northeast Africa from natives of that region. He also used Arab sources, as shown

Fig. 8. *In the fifteenth century, Europeans commonly believed the Indian Ocean to be an enclosed sea, as shown in the undated Berlinghieri edition of Ptolemy. Since the trade-rich Spice Islands appeared to be out of reach of European sailors, European traders had to depend on (and lose profits to) middlemen who operated overland caravans. Portuguese navigator Vasco da Gama's epochal voyage around the southern end of Africa between 1497 and 1499 punctured this myth of global geography. (Reproduced from the collections of the Library of Congress.)*

in his place-names on the coast of Africa, where Arab traders had been active for centuries. He may have been in contact with members of the Coptic Church from Ethiopia who had visited Venice. Some of the African names shown

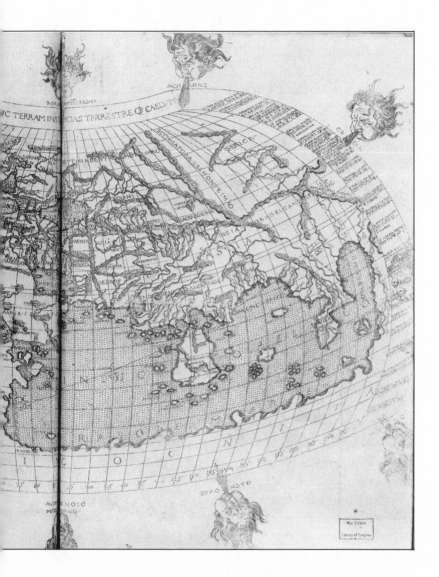

on Mauro's map are of Arabic origin, such as Maabase-Mombasa. His map indicated that the Indian Ocean was not enclosed but was navigable as a sea, a major breakthrough that may have derived from Arab sources and that Dias would confirm eighteen years later. In a rare break with verisimilitude, he showed Prester John's kingdom—in Ethiopia.

Portolans, although much more specialized than land maps, had always been more accurate simply because they were based on direct observation and on the use of the mariner's compass. In European maps, these books of sailing directions often showed the only features of foreign countries that were reliably depicted: the coasts. The charts were mandatory for mariners who plied the trade routes of the Mediterranean and the Indian Ocean. Portolans reached new levels of precision during the heyday of Genoese and Venetian trading activity. During the fourteenth century, mapmakers working in those two cities and in Amalfi and Pisa started to develop the commercial aspects of their craft. The founding and spread of the Islamic empire had helped coordinate and expand Arabic ocean trade, which reached from Africa to China. The earliest extant Arabic portolan, the Maghreb Chart, dates from around 1330 and features a mixed toponymy of names in Arabic, Italian, Catalan, and Spanish, a clear indication of the cross-cultural sources of information. In the 1400s, a growing body of Arabic navigational literature offered practical advice for navigators and pilots, especially in the Indian Ocean and the China Sea.

Pilots and cartographers routinely passed from the service of one nation or king to another. In 1512, for example, the Portuguese obtained a chart in Javanese that showed the Cape of Good Hope, Brazil, the Red Sea, the Persian Sea, and the Spice Islands and included accurate Chinese navigational plots. In China, Jesuit missionaries long played a role in exchanging information between the West and the East, particularly during the sixteenth century. An atlas of the provinces of China, compiled by Chu Ssu-pen between 1311 and 1312, was the model for the Jesuit Martino Marini's *Atlas Sinensism*, published in Amsterdam in 1737. In the early 1600s, the Polish missionary Michael Boym became the first European cartographer to insert Chinese characters and their nearest equivalent in Roman characters on a map of China; his map was reprinted in Paris three years later.

Although accurate data concerning Far Eastern geography trickled into Europe, details were wildly inconsistent when the first European maps of China appeared in the 1580s. Some showed the country to be the same size as Europe, others four or five times as large. Some maps treated China and Cathay as separate countries, although the Jesuits had shown they were the same. Mapmakers typically depicted China with five huge lakes, four in the interior and one on the western boundary. Although each lake was carefully named, none actually existed.

The European revival of Ptolemy, after an eclipse of more than a millennium, provided another impetus toward accuracy. In 1400, a Florentine scholar obtained the Greek text of Ptolemy's writings from Constantinople and translated it into Latin. The text and maps may have been reassembled in the tenth or eleventh century, perhaps by a Byzantine scribe, and Ptolemy's maps were redrawn based on his effort. From 1470 to 1500, different editions appeared simultaneously. With the publication of the German edition of Ptolemy's *Geography* in Strasbourg in 1513, the ancient astronomer reached the acme of his influence on cartography: his work served as the basis for a map of the world remarkable for being the first to show the New World separated from Asia.

The biggest problems posed by the renewal of Ptolemy's theories were the size of the earth and the relative sizes of continents and oceans. Ptolemy's calculations influenced mapmakers such as Martin Behaim, who combined voyages of exploration with commercial cartography. Behaim produced a globe during a stay in Nuremberg in 1490. If he had subtracted 46 degrees from Ptolemy's measure of 177 degrees for the extent of the Old World, Behaim would have been on the mark. Instead, he made it worse by *adding* 57 degrees, nearly cutting in half the distance from Europe west to Asia. Small wonder that the first explorers who crossed the Atlantic expected to pull up after a matter of weeks in an Indian or Chinese archipelago.

Although there is no evidence that Christopher Columbus used Behaim's map, both men had access to the same source materials and shared a similar view of the world. Planning his voyage across the Atlantic during the 1480s, Columbus studied a book by the French cosmographer Pierre d'Ailly, who in 1410 had also vastly underestimated the width of the Atlantic. Columbus's interest in d'Ailly's calculation is apparent in the underlined passages and marginal notes in his edition of the book. Columbus made Asia 283 degrees wide and added another 9 degrees for the Canaries (his point of departure), leaving just 68 degrees of ocean to cross. He also shrank the size of a degree, choosing the estimate of a medieval Muslim geographer and ending up with an estimated 4,300 kilometers of open water, less than a third of the actual distance to the real Indies. Somehow, he managed to come up with a decent estimate of the actual distance from Spain to the West Indies.

Explorers themselves, as noted earlier, proved to be dubious sources of information for mapmakers. They sometimes reported finding what they were looking for, not what they actually found. When Alessandro Zorzi mapped Columbus's own version of his discoveries, Zorzi showed them to be part of Asia, because of Columbus's refusal to believe he had discovered a new continent. Cartographers

54

DEREK NELSON

and scholars generally found it difficult to divorce the eastern lands (so convincingly described by Marco Polo) and the western discoveries of Columbus; new maps repeatedly superimposed these continents, often with the Asian mainland greatly extended to accommodate the data. Columbus took Cuba for an Oriental land (probably Japan) long known as Cipangu or, as on Fra Mauro's map, Zimpangu, but he later decided it was so large that it had to be Cathay. This notion was reflected on a 1506 map that shows Zimpangu and Hispaniola as the same island, located 50 degrees east of Asia. On his second voyage, Columbus took sworn statements from his officers that Cuba was a peninsula, the southeast promontory of Asia. On his final voyage, sailing the coast of Central America, he assumed that he had found Catigara (an ancient name for Indochina) and that he was just nineteen days' journey from the Ganges.

Columbus provided the beginning of a flood of information that would finally begin to establish the true outlines of the continents. Until that time, the market for maps in Europe was small, specialized, and rarely competitive. It included kings, travelers, statesmen, merchants, and scholars. Similarly, the Arabic map audience was made up of astronomers, astrologers, sea captains, and political rulers, along with a small, literate, cosmopolitan elite. What business existed for chart publishers was aimed at merchants. For the general public, commercial maps were a minor offshoot of the book trade and often included out-of-date information. The discoveries of Dias in 1487, Columbus in 1493, da Gama in India in 1498, and Cabral in Brazil in 1500 triggered unprecedented public interest. Although these new discoveries didn't appear in editions of Ptolemy until 1507 (perhaps the result of official censorship), the market demanded timely information.

Until the late 1400s, maps had to be slowly copied by hand. The advent both of the copperplate, which superseded the woodcut (the previous medium for map reproduction), and of printing and engraving, at the dawn of the sixteenth century, greatly increased distribution. Once these new technologies developed, the world was ready for the modern atlas: comprehensive, up-to-date, and convenient. Two cartographers, Abraham Ortelius and Gerardus Mercator, stood ready to supply it.

Ortelius was a new kind of mapmaker, a far cry from the cloistered monks and impractical theoreticians common in medieval times. He was a Flemish scholar, craftsman, and businessman, more an editor and publisher than a practical cartographer. In 1570, he issued his *Theatrum Orbis Terrarum*, containing seventy maps (fifty-six were of Europe). He acknowledged the work of eighty-seven cartographers in his first edition, a number that had more than doubled by the 1603 edition. By 1612, the atlas had gone through forty editions, in Latin, Dutch, German, French, Spanish, Italian, and English.

Mercator started out making mathematical and astronomical instruments and working as a land surveyor. He made his first map of the world in 1538, based on the work of Ptolemy. His patron was Charles V, Holy Roman emperor from 1519 to 1558, a man who had inherited an immense empire spanning Europe and Spanish America and who dreamed of making that empire universal. Wars with France and the advance of the Ottoman Turks thwarted the imperialist dreams of Charles V, but at his court, Mercator met navigators and cartographers from Portugal and Spain, then at the vanguard of exploration. Mercator's development of his own projection, in 1568, made him the foremost geographer and cartographer of his day.

Despite keeping to Ptolemy's underestimation of the earth's circumference and the error of showing the southern continent of Terra Australis covering the pole and reaching the southern tips of Africa and Asia, as well as including spurious landfalls such as Saint Brendan's Islands, Mercator was conscientious and continued to improve his maps. He also discarded many medieval misconceptions, reducing the length of the Mediterranean to the correct size, for example, and locating the Canary Islands in the right spot. His atlas proved extremely successful, going through forty-seven editions between 1595 and 1642.

In 1497, when the English explorer John Cabot reached what we now know as either Newfoundland or Nova Scotia, he thought he had found Asia and returned claiming to have visited the land of the great Khan. When navigators and mapmakers could no longer deny that it had to be recognized as a new continent, North America wasn't at first a goal in and of itself; it was a roadblock in the path of seafaring nations that wanted a piece of the lucrative Eastern trade. Spain and Portugal had already claimed the southern sea routes to the Far East. Latecomers had to find a way to the Pacific, and then to Cathay and the Spice Islands. The way lay either around or across North America, and everyone wanted to find it. The headlong quest for this strait would obsess adventurers from the sixteenth through the eighteenth centuries. Plenty of maps seemed to offer hope. Michael Lok's map of North America, published in 1582, shows Canada (above what is roughly the current United States, encompassing what Lok labeled "Florida" and "Apal chen") as a motley assortment of huge islands and loosely connected peninsulas.

During his voyages from 1576 to 1578, Martin Frobisher

57

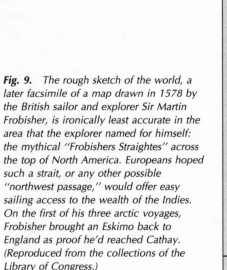

Fig. 9. *The rough sketch of the world, a later facsimile of a map drawn in 1578 by the British sailor and explorer Sir Martin Frobisher, is ironically least accurate in the area that the explorer named for himself: the mythical "Frobishers Straightes" across the top of North America. Europeans hoped such a strait, or any other possible "northwest passage," would offer easy sailing access to the wealth of the Indies. On the first of his three arctic voyages, Frobisher brought an Eskimo back to England as proof he'd reached Cathay. (Reproduced from the collections of the Library of Congress.)*

sailed 200 miles into Hudson Bay, searching for a supposed strait into the South Seas. His discoveries appeared in a contemporary chart as the "Mistaken Straightes." In 1610, Henry Hudson gave his name to the bay while seeking a short route to the Orient. Exploring the coast of North America for France, the Italian navigator Giovanni da Verrazano made landfall at Cape Fear, North Carolina, in March 1525, then headed north. He reported, somewhere south of Norombega (an ancient name for the territory that is now New England), a "little neck of lande" that divided the Atlantic from what he modestly called the Sea of Ver-

NORTH.
Polus Arcticus.

SEP=   TRIONA=   LIS.

Circulus arcticus

tartaria

EVROPA   ASIA   chin

Oceanus orientalis

Mare Mediterraneum   mare caspium

Mare atlanticus   India   Mare Eoum

AFRICA   Arabia   tropicus Cancri

guinea   Red Sea   calecut

Circulus aequinoctialis

brasil   montes Lunae   y. S. Lawrentÿ   Iava maior

Oceanus   Australis   tropicus Capricorni

capo di buona speranza

Magellanes

a del fuego

A V S T R A L I S.

Polus Antarticus.

EAST

the WORLD *M. Frobisher 1578.*

razano and that "bathed the limits of India, China, and Cathay." Verrazano was probably scanning the Outer Banks of North Carolina and Pamlico Sound, which today bathes the limits of such nonoriental places as Manteo, Wanchese, and Stumpy Point. Thereafter, a century of maps showed the New World shaped like an hourglass, with the Sea (or Gulf) of Verrazano the narrowest part.

Another version of this fictional sea appeared on a chart of Virginia in 1651. It showed Cape Hatteras, the Chesapeake Bay, and what is now roughly the states of North Carolina, Virginia, and Maryland inland to the mountains.

On the other side of these land areas is a body of water labeled the "Sea of China," and beyond that lay the Indies.

Still battling the mounting evidence, mapmakers pushed the imaginary sea farther and farther west. Pierre de la Verendrye, one of the leading Canadian explorers of the Rockies, moved it to the Missouri River on an expedition in 1731, and on to the Rocky Mountains in 1749. His reports forced the sea to migrate so far west that it linked up with another famous myth, the Strait of Juan de Fuca, a geographic obsession of the late 1600s and 1700s. The strait was named after a Spanish sailor who had reputedly found and explored it in 1592. R. A. Skelton traced the myth to a London magazine in 1708, which printed the story of a Spanish admiral who had supposedly sailed northwest via rivers and lakes from Chile, ultimately meeting a ship from Boston.

The growth of accurate geographic knowledge in Europe chased Prester John's fabulous empire across the ocean to the New World. Among the vast riches of his domain was an elixir that prevented aging, a tale that, according to some accounts, the Spanish explorer Juan Ponce de León, among others, was said to have heard from Caribs. He may have been keeping an eye out for a fountain of everlasting youth as he voyaged in search of Bimini in 1513.

The fable of the seven golden cities of Cibola was launched by Marcos de Niza, a Franciscan friar and explorer in Spanish North America, who headed a 1539 expedition from Mexico upon hearing Zuñi stories of rich pueblos. De Niza headed north into Arizona, issuing reports that were erroneous but enthusiastic. The British Museum has an anonymous, undated map, estimated to have been drawn in the early 1500s, that shows Cibola along the East Coast of North America, in present-day South Carolina.

The legend of El Hombre Dorado, the "golden man,"

described a sacred lake into which a king, covered with powdered gold, hurled bullion and emeralds as gifts to the gods. Stories of this ceremony persisted for centuries. Natives in the New World learned to fan the flames of European greed, regaling the Spanish with stories that featured lots of precious metal, located somewhere over the horizon. When reporting back to headquarters, the explorers themselves were no more reliable. In 1595, when Sir Walter Raleigh sailed up the Orinoco River in Guiana, he returned with tales of monsters, of the "rich and beautiful Empier of Guiana," and of the "great and golden Citie, which the Spaniards call El Dorado, and the naturals Manoa."

Columbus, who believed that Saint Brendan's Island existed, searched for it during his first voyage. Diego Velasquez, governor of Cuba during the Spanish conquest in the 1520s, told the Spanish conquistador Hernando Cortez to be on the lookout for such creatures as the Panoti, a race whose ears were large enough to serve as blankets, and the Cynocephali, who had the heads of dogs. In 1522, Cortez collected bones he took to be those of the giants described by Pliny and shipped them back to Charles V. Magellan thought he spotted dog-headed people, dressed in animal skins, in Argentina. To name them, he chose the Spanish word *Patagon*, the name of a dog-headed monster in a sixteenth-century Spanish romance. The name also came to refer to the giants who reportedly inhabited the region. Antonio Pigafeta, a member of Magellan's expedition, recorded that they saw a naked giant on the beach, so tall that a human reached only to its waist. Soon, maps showed two giants along with a normal-sized person in a place called Tierra de Patagones, at the southern end of South America.

History resolved these myths in odd ways. Sebastian

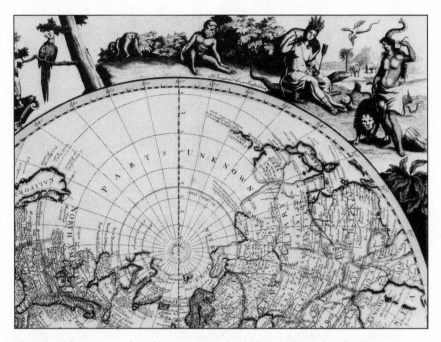

Fig. 10. *Information gathered by mariners helped fill in the coastal outlines on maps first; the mysterious inner regions sometimes remained populated by imaginary monsters. Early sixteenth-century maps showed huge areas of "unknown land" in South America, where such prominent explorers as Magellan expected to find dog-headed people and 10-foot-tall giants. This 1714 map shows an equivalent "parts unknown" in modern-day Canada and Siberia. (Reproduced from the collections of the Library of Congress.)*

Cabot had accompanied his father, John, on what may have been the European discovery of Canada in 1497. In the late 1520s, trying to reach the Indies on behalf of the Spanish, he essayed a southern route, eventually encountering natives in South America who had gold and silver ornaments. Cabot hoped that meant El Dorado was not too far in the country's interior and even named the nearby river Rio de la Plata, the "river of plate." That christening did not transform the mythical city into reality, however. The lustrous legend of "El Dorado" gradually tarnished,

DEREK NELSON

Fig. 11. *Equipped with a splendid map such as this one from 1601, what explorer could doubt the existence of giants in South America? The mythical Patagonian giants were a staple of maps and travel books for centuries. (Reproduced from the collections of the Library of Congress.)*

and the term came to mean an impossible quest. Nevertheless, it eventually found its way into modern atlases and gazetteers. There is an El Dorado in Arkansas and an Eldorado in Kansas (named in the 1860s because the town's founders beheld a gorgeous sunset on the day they arrived), among others.

Beginning in the mid-1500s, maps of the North Atlantic or the northern polar regions showed another mythical place called Friesland, usually located southeast of Greenland. The fiction lasted for a century, until it eventually proved to be the creation of Nicolo Zeno, a Venetian map publisher, but today, Friesland (or Frisia) is the name of a province in the northern part of the Netherlands.

Although no one ever found the Fountain of Youth, search as they might in Florida and the Caribbean, the Isle of Youth is the name of one of the lesser-known Cuban islands. The mythical Strait of Juan de Fuca also became a real place, lying between Vancouver Island in Canada and the northwest tip of Washington State, but it flows only 100 miles toward the Atlantic, never reaching the ocean, as once was fabled. Ptolemy's Mountains of the Moon appear only in geographical dictionaries, which identify them as part of the Ruwenzori mountain group in central Africa between Lake Albert (called Lake Mobutu Sese Seko since 1973) and Lake Edward (temporarily called Lake Idi Amin Dada in the 1970s) on the boundary between Uganda and Zaire. In 1858, J. H. Speke determined the source of the Nile to be Lake Victoria.

Mapmakers eventually decided that the Fortunate Isles were the Canary Islands and the Madeira group, but other ancient legends flicker in our peripheral vision. When I requested information about the origins of the name of Bahrain (a country of thirty-three islands in the Arabian Gulf, east of Saudi Arabia), the staff of its United Nations mission sent a brochure that said the country may have been the site of Dilmun (the "land of immortality"), described in Sumerian, Babylonian, and Assyrian inscriptions as a major port of call on sea trade routes between Mesopotamia and India. The staff at the Zimbabwe mission to the United Nations suggests that Zimbabwe is the ancient land of

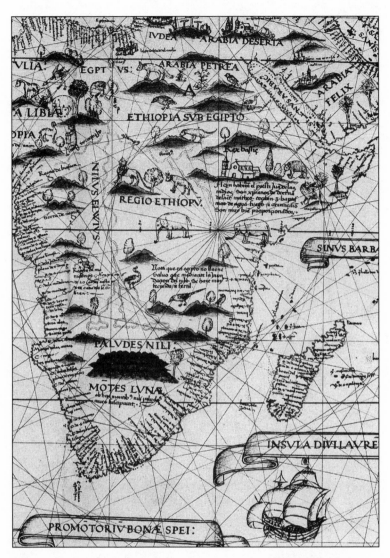

Fig. 12. *During the second century A.D., the Greco-Egyptian scholar Ptolemy decided that the Nile originated in a place he called the Mountains of the Moon in southern Africa, here shown as Motes Luna on a 1529 map. More than a thousand years later, numerous explorers took his word for it and trekked off through dense African jungles looking for the mountains. Ptolemy may have been referring to the Ruwenzori mountain range in east central Africa. Its peaks reach above 16,000 feet and are usually blanketed with mist. (Reproduced from the collections of the Library of Congress.)*

65

Ophir, which the Bible mentions as the site of King Solomon's mines. According to a pamphlet from the Kenya National Tourist Office, "Man was born on the eastern shore of Lake Rudolf, according to recent fossil evidence. And the implication is that Kenya was the Biblical Garden of Eden . . ."

Some mythical place-names found a new home on Mars. The Italian astronomer Giovanni Schiaparelli, famous for announcing the finding of *canali* (canals or channels) on Mars in 1877, which proved to be an illusion, applied classic names from geography and mythology to features on the planet. Many names, such as Utopia and Hesperia, have been approved by the International Astronomical Union, governing body for names in space. Others, including Eden and Chaos, have not been sanctioned.

The Northwest Passage, long shown on maps that were incorrect and optimistic, then discarded for two centuries, was finally established through the Arctic in 1819–20, when ships reached Viscount Melville Sound in Canada's Northwest Territories from both the east and the west. An ice-breaking tanker, the SS *Manhattan*, became the first commercial ship to make the transit in 1969, more than three centuries after the first tentative explorations.

Despite our immense resources, not all modern maps are correct or readily understood. At the beginning of World War II, an official army map showed Stalingrad on the wrong river. Maps in newspapers have shown part of Michigan in Wisconsin, Virginia's Delmarva Peninsula as part of Maryland, and both North and South Korea as part of the Soviet Union. The Arizona Department of Transportation omitted Mesa, the state's third largest city, from its most recent map. And what would Mercator have made of the British maps that repeat Australia and New Zealand at both the left and right sides?

In early 1990, the Alaska legislature launched a campaign to persuade national newspapers, magazines, and textbook publishers to start showing Alaska in the correct geographical position on maps of the United States. Schoolchildren in the lower forty-eight states commonly mistake it for an island south of California, because most maps save space by depicting it that way, also greatly shrinking the state, which is actually about one-fifth the size of the rest of the United States.

Cartographic fantasy hasn't vanished, either, and George Demko has the files to prove it. Demko headed the State Department's Office of the Geographer, the department's research and advisory arm, during the 1980s (he now teaches geography at Dartmouth College). For his amusement, he kept a file called "Mythical Kingdoms, Kooky Kings and Pretending Princes." He recorded such self-declared places as the Realm of Redonda, a pile of rocks off Bermuda, which flew pajama bottoms as its flag. In 1948, a group of fishermen proclaimed a small island off Nova Scotia to be the Principality of Outer Baldonia. As an independent nation, its citizens could drink, cuss, and gamble without restriction. Thus do the fabulous kingdom of Prester John and the not-quite-immortal Islands of Saint Brendan find modern parallels.

WHY SOME NAMES
SEEM TO MISS
THE TARGET

The Rocky Mountains form the stone spine of North America; Liberia was an African homeland for freed slaves. For each of these straightforward names, though, there is one that puzzles. Cape Verde is Portuguese for "green cape," except the fifteen stark, volcanic islands aren't in the least verdant. But to those Portuguese explorers, who expected to find a world burned crisp by the sun once they sailed past the Saharan coast of Africa, they seemed lush enough. In fact, rainfall is scant and the islands are plagued with drought and famine. Only 10 percent of the land is arable, and even that land is infertile.

Liberia's neighbor to the north, Sierra Leone (lion ridge) was named by Portuguese explorers in 1460. The peninsula where they landed is indeed mountainous, but later researchers deduced that the Portuguese saw billowing cu-

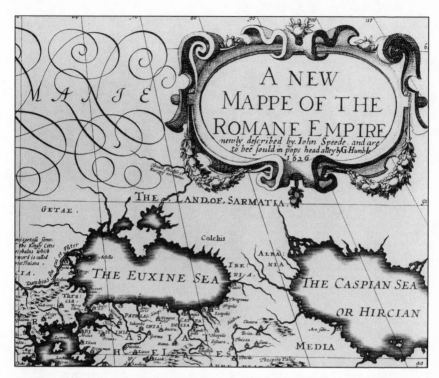

Fig. 13. *The name of the Euxine Sea (left) derives from the old Latin name for the Black Sea: Pontus Euxinus, meaning "hospitable." The name seems ill-fitting, since the sea was known for its fierce storms and rocky coast. (Reproduced from the collections of the Library of Congress.)*

mulus clouds, not mountain peaks. In any case, the roaring they heard was either thunder or pounding surf, definitely not the king of beasts.

At first glance, the old Japanese name for America, Bei-koku—literally, "rice country"—is absurd. It turns out, however, the Japanese term is taken from a Chinese character rendering a phonetic spelling of America that has nothing to do with rice. During the Roman Empire, the Latin name for the Black Sea was Pontus Euxinus, "hospitable," yet the sea was noted for storms and rock-strewn

DEREK NELSON

shorelines. One source says that the Romans disliked its original Greek name, Axinos, which means "inhospitable."

Wyoming comes from the Algonquian Mache-weaming, "place of the big flats" or "large prairie place." The name in turn came from the Wyoming Valley in western Pennsylvania, site of a prerevolutionary massacre of native Americans. James M. Ashley, an Ohio congressman who chaired the Committee on Territories, chose it when the Wyoming Territory was organized in 1868 because he thought it sounded "beautiful"; several U.S. counties share it. Although Wyoming does have prairies, its highest mountain peaks, which tower over 13,000 feet, are more prominent features.

Why did two continents end up being named for Amerigo Vespucci? In 1499, he sailed to the New World with Spanish conquistador Alonso de Ojeda, who had been on Columbus's second voyage. Vespucci parted company with Ojeda before land was sighted. He headed his ship south, discovering and exploring the mouth of the Amazon, then cruising the northern shore of South America. He returned to Spain in 1500, sailed west again for the Portuguese in 1501, and returned to serve the Spanish, who made him the country's pilot major. He ultimately examined a total of 6,000 miles of the southern coast of South America. If explorers were ranked by the amount of coast they navigated, Vespucci would be near the top.

Although he was later lambasted for self-glorification, he didn't presume to name a continent after himself. The culprit was Martin Waldseemüller, who, along with a colleague, Philesius Ringmann, published *Cosmographiae Introductio* in 1507, which included a commentary on Vespucci's discoveries. Vespucci had written a series of accounts describing his voyages to what he called the "new

world.'' Some of the narratives were rewritten and sensationalized by an unknown author, who published them under the title *Four Voyages*. Waldseemüller read this book and, apparently under the impression that Vespucci had discovered the South American continent, attached the Latinized version of Vespucci's first name to the rough representation of South America in his maps. He credited Columbus's discoveries in another section. The publisher

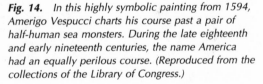

Fig. 14. *In this highly symbolic painting from 1594, Amerigo Vespucci charts his course past a pair of half-human sea monsters. During the late eighteenth and early nineteenth centuries, the name America had an equally perilous course. (Reproduced from the collections of the Library of Congress.)*

issued two editions of *Cosmographiae Introductio*, responding to brisk sales that amounted to thousands of copies in Europe.

After further research, Waldseemüller realized that he had erroneously honored Vespucci. He deleted the name in later editions, but he didn't offer any replacement. By then the name had gained widespread usage. In 1538, Mercator further cemented the naming by including it in his immensely influential series of maps and, as an after-thought, extending the name to North America.

Vespucci was the first to recognize that South America was a separate continent, yet scholars and others derided his accomplishments. The American poet and essayist Ralph Waldo Emerson, scarcely a muckraker, wrote in *English Traits* in 1856: "Strange that broad America was to wear the name of a thief! Amerigo Vespucci, the pickle-dealer at Seville, who went out in 1499, a subaltern with Hojeda, and whose highest naval rank was boatswain's mate, in an expedition that never sailed, managed in this lying world to supplant Columbus, and baptize half the earth with his name!" Emerson's reference to a supposedly phony expedition refers to questions about the authenticity of the original voyage. Vespucci's reputation wasn't effectively rehabilitated until the 1920s and 1930s.

Perhaps the name America took hold because the alliteration was irresistible when the new continents were listed along with Asia and Africa. Cartographers nevertheless tried out a variety of short-lived alternatives. A world map drawn during the mid-1500s showed the name Terra de Cuba for North America, and the name Isabella for Cuba. In his book of maps printed in London in 1627, English cartographer John Speed showed the two continents as "North America or Mexicana" and "South America or Peru." In 1902, the staff of the National Geographic Society reported the discovery of a 1516 copy of a Waldseemüller map on which South America was labeled "Brazilia sive Terra Papagalli" (Brazil, the land of parrots). As we saw on an earlier map, the name Brasil had already been assigned to an island (later proven to be imaginary) somewhere in the Atlantic.

It was Thomas Paine who coined the formal name for the new nation that emerged from the former British col-

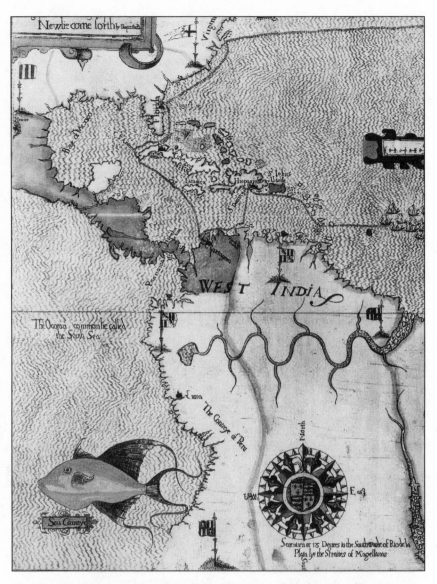

Fig. 15. *The place-name legacy of Columbus's classic gaffe is shown on this 1588 map as a country at the top of South America. Note that the names Florida and Virginia have already appeared. (Reproduced from the collections of the Library of Congress.)*

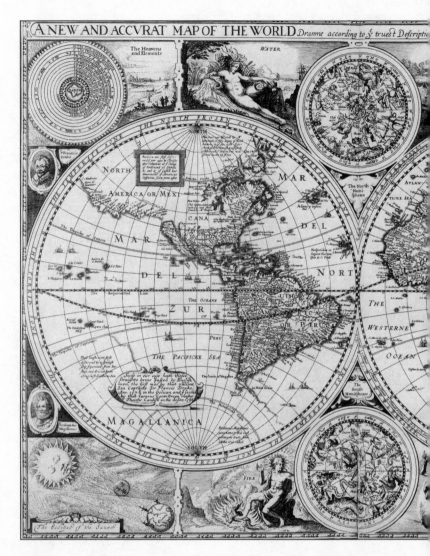

A NEW AND ACCVRAT MAP OF THE WORLD *Drawne according to y̆ truest Descriptio*

onies: the United States of America. It occurs in the pre-
amble to the Declaration of Independence. Until the
Articles of Confederation were ratified in 1781, the country
was also called the Congress; the Articles refer to it as "The
United States in Congress Assembled." The phrase "united

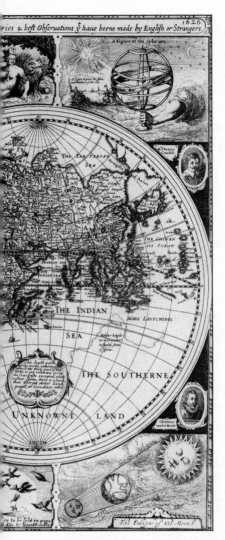

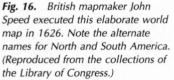

Fig. 16. British mapmaker John Speed executed this elaborate world map in 1626. Note the alternate names for North and South America. (Reproduced from the collections of the Library of Congress.)

states" is less a name than a political definition and had been used by the kingdom of Holland between 1617 and 1769, by Mexico, and by at least two South American countries. It troubled some of the early American federalists, who wanted a single name that truly unified the nation. The standing reference to states, in the plural, seemed to imply the possibility of future separation, which the Civil War would later prove well-founded. Furthermore, calling the people of the United States "Americans" was problematic because the residents of Central and South America were equally American.

A rival name for North America appeared on a 1570 map: Columbana. America referred only to South America. The suggestion was revived by the American poet and journalist Philip Freneau, who, penning one of his powerful pieces of propaganda in support of the Revolution, wrote in *American Liberty* in 1775: "What madness, heaven, had made Britannia frown?/ Who plans or schemes to pull Columbia down?" Popular imagination did not embrace Columbus as a hero prior to the Revolutionary War. British writers and historians emphasized the Cabots' rediscovery of North America. After the war, however, the Cabots were too closely associated with the British king for whom they had sailed, and Columbus offered a patriotic alternative.

Sporadic proposals to rename the country after the Norse voyager Leif Eriksson, who visited what was probably either New England or Nova Scotia in A.D. 1000 after being blown off course on a voyage from Norway to Greenland, never gained serious attention. In 1800, Fredonia was floated as a contender, eventually becoming adopted by several new towns, and in the 1933 film *Duck Soup*, the Marx Brothers used it as the name of an impoverished duchy. The American author and diplomat Washington Irving proposed Appalachia or Alleghania, based on native names.

Stubbornly honoring Columbus, Spanish politicians and mapmakers referred to the New World as Columbia throughout the eighteenth century. The name went to the capital of South Carolina in 1786, to the country at the top of South America, and, in 1858, to British Columbia in western Canada when it was an unorganized territory in the throes of a gold rush. In the United States, Columbus's name was also given to the nation's capital, the District of Columbia, and Columbia developed as a feminine symbol for America, sometimes called Lady Liberty.

The conventional explanation of Greenland's name is that Erik the Red, circa A.D. 982, bestowed it in an effort to lure colonists to a forbidding landscape. Most etymologists aren't convinced by the evidence for this theory. There are ancient geographic references to an island in the North Atlantic called Cronos, a name that may have undergone a linguistic transition to Cronia to Cronland to Gronland. It is possible that when Erik the Red landed on Greenland, he assumed that it was this previously identified island. Another piece of the puzzle fell into place in 1194, when an Icelandic voyager discovered land somewhere to the north of Greenland and named it Svalbard. It is part of the Arctic Archipelago, equidistant from Norway and Greenland. Later research showed that the Icelander's "discovery" was probably part of the east coast of Greenland. Svalbard—the real one—wended its way back into the saga in 1435, when Russian colonists arrived there.

In 1500, Portugal's King Manuel I sent explorer Gaspar Corte-Real to search for the Northwest Passage, a strait through North America to the Indies. Although the evidence is inconclusive that Corte-Real actually landed on Greenland, his voyage reminded mapmakers about that huge island, and it began reappearing on maps of the Atlantic. Cartographers began translating "green land" into

Fig. 17. *Greenland might as well have been a gigantic floating island during the Middle Ages for all that most mapmakers knew of it. They showed it attached to the Old World, the New World, and in many North Atlantic locations in between. In this 1513 edition of Ptolemy, its location approximates where Scandinavia is today. (Reproduced from the collections of the Library of Congress.)*

their own languages, spelling it Groenland or Gronland or Engroenland. Such translation sometimes spawned a mysterious Green Island on maps (also called Isla Verde or Insula Veridis) in the North Atlantic. Some maps treated Svalbard as part of Greenland; others showed it as part of northern Europe, adjacent to Russia. The mid-1500s produced numerous accounts of voyages to both places, which assumed various names, but sometimes they were treated as one place. Maps generally showed Greenland and Spitsbergen (the largest island in the Svalbard archipelago) as connected. The Dutch navigator Willem Barents rediscovered the real Greenland in 1596, and British explorers Martin Frobisher and John Davis visited in the late sixteenth century. As late as 1675, however, a map by cartographer Joseph Moxon labeled the actual Greenland as Groenlandia and Spitsbergen as Greenland.

The climax came in the 1890s, when, on the strength of the 1194 "discovery" of Svalbard, the government of Norway determined that it had actually been Spitsbergen and therefore Norwegian property, a claim highly doubtful to many geographers but ratified by the League of Nations in 1925.

The conventional wisdom is that Greenland should have been called Iceland and vice versa. More than four-fifths of Greenland's 840,000 square miles are covered with ice, some of it nearly three miles deep. The nation has no forests, and less than 1 percent is under cultivation. And while roughly one-quarter of Iceland is grassy and habitable, much of it is barren as well (the north and east are polar and tundralike). Some historians identify Iceland with a place the Greeks called Ultima Thule, after a navigator named Pytheas discovered it circa 310 B.C. (Ultima Thule might have been Norway or the Shetland Islands off northern Scotland.) Today, Thule is a real town and a district in—to keep matters confusing—Greenland.

It is tempting to attack the names bestowed by European explorers, especially because some of them were given in a cavalier manner. As C. M. Matthews wrote in *Place Names of the English-Speaking World,* Columbus "had to the highest degree that arrogance, common among explorers, which made them feel that anything they found was theirs to name regardless of its own life and history." Columbus had no qualms about assigning names based on nothing more than whim.

In 1855, David Livingstone arrived at a mile-wide break in the 1,700-mile-long Zambezi River. The water plunges 420 feet, churning up a thick mist and producing a roar that can be heard 25 miles away. It is the world's greatest waterfall, more than twice as wide and deep as Niagara. He wrote in his journal: "On sights as beautiful as this, angels in their flight must have gazed." It had a fine name already: Mose-oa-Tunya, "smoke that thunders," but Livingstone chose to name it after Queen Victoria. Should the name be discarded, and the older one restored?

Marcel Aurousseau, secretary of the Permanent Committee on Geographic Names for British Official Use from 1936 to 1955, had no fondness for native names. Writing in *The Rendering of Geographical Names,* published in 1957, he regretted the loss of the name Sandwich Islands. James Cook named the Hawaiian islands after John Montagu, fourth earl of Sandwich, who served three times as first lord of the admiralty. Montagu's reputation suffered during the humiliating defeats of the American Revolution, however, and today he is better known as the inventor of the handy meal that bears his name. (He created it as something to eat while gambling, so he wouldn't have to take a break from the table.) Not surprisingly, British influence on the islands was weak.

After charting parts of New England, Captain John Smith asked fifteen-year-old Prince Charles to exchange the Indians' "barbarous names" for English ones. Thus Accomminticus became Boston (not the well-known one in Massachusetts, but the city that is now York, Maine), and Accomack became Plimouth (later, Plymouth). On his own initiative, Smith gave the name Tragabigzanda to a cape, in honor of a Turkish woman who had befriended him when he was enslaved by the Indians; it later became Cape Anna.

An entry in the 1874 *Imperial Gazetteer* lists Murder Island in the Mozambique Channel, three miles off the southwest coast of Madagascar. The name was given "by Captain Owen, in consequence of the murder there of two of his midshipmen by the natives." The text adds, "See First Island," implying a later, understandable name change.

Niue, an island dependency of New Zealand, was once called Savage Island. On December 13, 1642, while sailing for the Dutch East India Company on a voyage of discovery in the South Seas, Dutch navigator Abel Janszoon Tasman skirted the island now named Tasmania. Winds sent his ships eastward, and he made landfall off Okarito on the western coast of New Zealand's South Island. Maoris in a canoe attacked one of his rowboats, killing three of Tasman's sailors. He named the place Moordenaars (murderers) Bay; it also appeared on maps as Massacre Bay but is now called Golden Bay.

The trend toward editing vivid place names out of existence appears global. In 1964, Belorussia changed the name of the town of Zagryazye (dirty place) to Bereznyanka (birch trees). Bermuda's Hog Island, northeast of New Providence Island, became Paradise Island in 1960. Admittedly, it would be hard to advertise Hog Island on a cruise ship's Caribbean itinerary. There is also a Hog Island in the Grenadines, off Grenada. This one is not exactly a tourist mecca, but it remains on the map.

Names are always in flux, but patterns are enigmatic. Perfectly good names get discarded by the first foreign explorer on the scene; fallacious names hang on for centuries. The whole process of assigning names is questionable. Does a name fit? Is it appropriate or misleading? If a name changes, is the new name better or worse? The existence of such queries reveals just how illogical some place-names are and how unpredictable is their survival.

DEREK NELSON

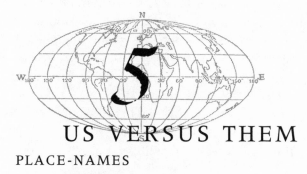

US VERSUS THEM

PLACE-NAMES
BECOME PEJORATIVE

Many tribes and communities around the globe refer to themselves by some variant of "the people" or "the men." They know who and where they are; the concepts of *us* and *here* are clear enough. It is others—neighboring tribes, foreign invaders, the inhabitants of the village down the road—who need description. In parts of New Guinea, people have names for nearby villages but not their own. The names neighboring communities give each other reflect the nature of their contact, sometimes betokening harmonious relations, more often revealing antagonisms that arise from competition over local resources. When trade and continental wars made distant nations into rivals, what had been local matters became global.

We use these freighted names without recognizing them for what they are, because we inherit them as part of our vocabulary; yet most are undeserved. The tribe we refer to as the Navaho called themselves Dine, "the people." The name Navaho comes from *tewa navaho* (great planted fields), a term used enviously to describe the land holdings of the wealthy, powerful Dine. So-called Eskimos don't like their given name because it comes from an Algonquian word meaning "eaters of raw flesh." Eskimo groups in Canada and Greenland prefer to call themselves Inuit, plural of *Inuk*, which means "person" or "man." The tribe we call the Sioux called themselves Dakotah, "the allies" (derived from *da*, "to think of as," and *koda*, "friend"). Rival tribes called them Nadowessioux, "little snakes" or "the enemy."

Few vacationers who visit New York's lovely Adirondack Mountains realize that the place-name comes from an insult aimed by the Mohawks at a tribe of Algonquian people who lived in the mountains in northeastern New York State. The Mohawks called them Hatiróntaks, meaning "leaf eaters" or "they eat trees," a mocking reference to the diet that allegedly resulted from a lack of skill in hunting. The name may have entered the English language by way of the Mohawks' alliance with the British.

When Saxons invaded England, they drove the Cymri (compatriots or brothers) into the western hills, calling them *weals* (foreigner) or *walas* (the enemy). This root word, incidentally, appears in German as *wal*, which led to words such as *walnut*, "foreign nut." The enmity between England and Wales harks back to two hundred years of guerrilla warfare between 800 and 1000. English rule was established in 1284, the Welsh rebelled in the fifteenth century, and nationalist agitation continues to this day. This animosity—not the comparative honesty of the Welsh people—explains the origin of the verb *to welsh*, meaning

Fig. 18. *Ferdinand Magellan bestowed the name Ladrones Islands, which means "thieves islands," after natives stole from his crew. The island group is in the northern Marianas (here shown in the upper quadrant of a map projection centered on the South Pole). The name is a classic example of a place-name that is little more than an insult. Although Spanish Jesuits restored the name Marianas in the mid-1600s, Magellan's version remained on maps as late as the eighteenth century. (Reproduced from the collections of the Library of Congress.)*

87

to swindle someone by reneging on a bet or failing to fulfill an obligation.

The conflict between England and Ireland is even older. The British conquered Ireland in 1171, triggering an 800-year struggle punctuated by numerous revolts. This bitter struggle produced more than a few examples of English sarcasm. The *Oxford English Dictionary* traces the term *Irish hurricane*, meaning dead calm, to 1827. Some terms derided the poverty of the Irish: *Irish draperies* were cobwebs, and an *Irish lantern* was the moon. When Irish immigrants crowded into New York City in the nineteenth and twentieth centuries, old-world rivalry and new competition produced new variations on this theme. The term *Irish confetti* (meaning rocks or bricks) was an American contribution, when the Irish arrived in great numbers in the aftermath of the potato famine.

British sailors had long referred to untidy, loose ropes in the rigging as *Irish pennants*. When the Netherlands became England's chief foe, the ropes became *Dutch pennants*. English derision of the Dutch stemmed from intense commercial rivalry in the seventeenth century, when the Dutch East India Company and Dutch West India Company traded on every continent, capturing the largest share of the world's seagoing trade. Wars with England from 1652 to 1654 and 1664 to 1667 made matters worse, as did the Dutch siding against England in the American Revolution. English speakers coined terms such as *Dutch courage* (bravery inspired by booze) and *in Dutch* (in trouble). A *Dutch nightingale* was a frog, and as early as 1887, if you went on a *Dutch treat*, you had to pay your own way. In 1934, the Dutch government judged the epithetic habit to be so ruinously ingrained that it ordered an official substitution of the word *Netherlands* for *Dutch*.

Others words, such as *barbarian*, may have started out

DEREK NELSON

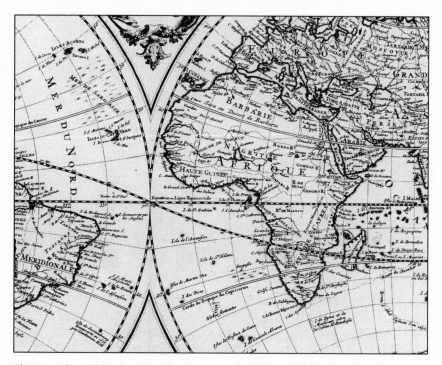

Fig. 19. The Barbary Coast's earlier name was Barbarie, which shares its linguistic roots with the word barber. The earliest barbarians were simply foreigners with beards, not people who were necessarily "barbaric" in the modern sense of the word. (Reproduced from the collections of the Library of Congress.)

as neutral descriptions. Barbaria appears on the Mediterranean coast of Africa on a map made between 1648 and 1665 by William Janszoon Blaeu, though its name is more familiar in a later version, the Barbary Coast. Since *barba* means "beard" in Latin, some sources suggest that clean-shaven Romans used the name for unshaven foreigners (the word *barber* derives from the same Latin root). The two concepts—*bearded* and *foreign*—gradually became synonymous, so the place-name Barbarie came to mean "foreign country," and *barbarian* meant "foreigner." At various times in ancient history, the term was applied to people who weren't Greek, or Roman, or Christian.

The Greek word *barbaros* added negative connotations such as rude, strange, or ignorant and, by the end of the seventeenth century, came to mean people who were wild and uncivilized. Later it also meant cruel and brutal. The Chinese applied it to Westerners beginning in the mid-nineteenth century.

The gradual intensifying of negative shades of meaning is only loosely related to Barbarie's history. The original Barbary States—Tripolitania, Tunisia, Algeria, and Morocco—developed as semiautonomous provinces of the Turkish Empire from the sixteenth through the nineteenth centuries. Pirates first sailed out of Barbary Coast ports during Turkey's sixteenth-century wars to prevent the region from falling into the hands of expansionist Spain. During the seventeenth and eighteenth centuries, the raids were less military and more commercial, aiming for booty, ransom, and slaves. In more recent times, the waterfront district in San Francisco was called the Barbary Coast in the late 1800s and was infamous for its saloons, gambling houses, and brothels.

Gypsies acquired their English-language name because they were once thought to have come from Egypt. In fact, they probably originated in northwest India and left their original homeland for Persia sometime after the birth of Christ, entering western Europe in the fifteenth century. They developed a unique language and culture, roaming in nomadic caravans of entertainers, metal workers, horse dealers, mechanics, and fortune tellers. The term *gypsy* came to mean a member of a wandering race, though by the sixteenth century it was no longer neutral, as evidenced by a quotation from the *Oxford English Dictionary* describing them as "a company of lewde personnes within the realm calling themselves Gipcyans." Gypsies reached North America in the 1800s, and by the 1930s, they had developed a notorious reputation in New York as con artists, specializing in fortune-telling scams. By then, the verb *to gyp*, which had entered American slang in the 1880s, certainly seemed appropriate. Etymologists, however, aren't certain that *gyp* did come from *gypsy*.

The French mistakenly thought that gypsies originated in Bohemia, a former Czech republic that probably lay along their route into Europe. The Bohemian kingdom, established in the ninth century, had a long, complex political and social history. The place-name became familiar to British readers via Arthur Conan Doyle's first Sherlock Holmes story, "A Scandal in Bohemia," published in *The Strand* magazine in July 1891. Holmes's client was Wilhelm Gottsreich Sigismond von Ormstein, grand duke of Cassel-Felstein and hereditary king of Bohemia, whose problem, Dr. Watson observed, "may have an influence upon European history." *Bohemian* hadn't acquired regal overtones, though—quite the reverse. As far back as the late seventeenth century, it described vagabonds, adventurers, and people with irregular habits who were unconventional. Perhaps unwittingly, Conan Doyle used this meaning of the word in the second paragraph of his story, writing that his fictional detective "loathed every form of society with his whole Bohemian soul." Sixty years later in the United States, the prevalent bohemians wore bearded, sandal-wearing beatniks.

The antisocial character traits ascribed to gypsies and bohemians had nothing to do, then, with the inhabitants of Egypt or Bohemia. The verb *to shanghai* had a slightly better rationale. How did this Chinese port become synonymous with nautical kidnapping? For centuries, press-gangs all over the world had gotten sailors drunk or knocked them out, then forced them into service aboard ships. In the nineteenth century, kidnapping sailors for voyages to the Orient came to be called "shipping a man to Shanghai." Shanghai dates from the eleventh century, but it only became important on the world scene after it was forcibly opened to foreign trade in 1842. One of the world's great harbors, it rapidly became a leading Chinese seaport and the nation's largest city. The verb *to shanghai* had entered nautical slang in the United States by 1871, when a *New York Tribune* journalist described some sailors who had become victims: ". . . they would have been drugged, shanghaied, and taken away from all means of making complaint." The meaning of the word soon embraced kidnapping and imprisonment.

Certainly sailors were shanghaied to Shanghai, but there is little reason to think that more kidnapped sailors ended up there than in Genoa or Macao. Perhaps the Chinese city's name evoked a sense of distance and danger that other seaports lacked. It may have been a generic example of a faraway place, like Tombouctou, and Western distrust of China may have made its use seem credible.

The term *philistine* derives from Philistia, an ancient confederacy of independent cities in southwestern Palestine. The cities' control of iron supplies and tight political organization made them anathema to the Jews, who failed to conquer them. As early as the 1600s, calling someone a philistine meant they were a natural or traditional enemy (the term was wittily applied to bailiffs and critics, for example). Then, in 1693, a German preacher used the word in a sermon at the funeral of a student who had been killed by townspeople. German university students began applying the term to townsmen in general, deriding them as uneducated. It came to mean crass, prosaic, and materialistic.

To American tourists, the Caribbean conjures serene

images of turquoise water lapping at white sand, palm trees silhouetted against tropical sunsets—about as far from flesh-eating savagery as one can imagine, yet that is what the first European explorers expected to find there. Anecdotal evidence of cannibalism appeared in many accounts of European encounters in the New World. Columbus based a typical report on an event that occurred during his second voyage to America, in November 1493. A landing party went ashore near the Virgin Islands, and a canoeful of natives attacked, killing a Spaniard with an arrow. It was the first time Columbus or his crew had encountered hostile natives. The Spaniards overpowered and captured them; their partly shaved heads, long black braids, and red-painted skin made a deep impression. Earlier, members of a tribe known as the Tainos had told Columbus that flesh-eaters lived on nearby islands and that they were called Caribs or Canibs (perhaps a local dialectic version of the same name). Columbus assumed that the Indians he had fought were these Caribs and that they ate human flesh. Vespucci reported spending twenty-seven days with cannibals in 1502 and buying ten captives to keep them from being slaughtered and eaten. Giovanni da Verrazano may have had a less agreeable experience. Looking for a way to Asia, he had explored the Atlantic coast of North America for France in the 1520s. In 1528, probing south of regions he'd visited earlier, he anchored off what was probably Guadeloupe. According to a story brought back by his brother, Verrazano went ashore, where he was attacked and eaten by cannibals.

World maps already showed cannibal tribes scattered throughout Africa and the Americas, sometimes with illustrations of natives gnawing human bones and cooking human flesh over bonfires. Whether the name was spelled Canibales, Canibas, or Caribas, it was gradually applied to

Fig. 20. *The words* cannibal *and* Caribbean *derive from the same tribal name, an Arawak word meaning "strong men" or "brave men." There is no documentation of actual flesh-eating in the region, but illustrations on maps were graphic and convincing. This 1532 view shows a charnel house–cum–butcher shop, staffed with naked savages. (Reproduced from the collections of the Library of Congress.)*

DEREK NELSON

the entire Atlantic region of Central America, becoming a synonym for man-eater. In fact, the name derived from an Arawak word meaning "strong men" or "brave men."

Modern anthropologists disagree whether cannibalism has ever been adequately documented in any society. Some researchers find that nearly all accounts are based on accusations by neighboring enemies, tales from ancestors, or accounts drawn from hearsay. Even those anthropologists who think that indigenous tribes engaged in cannibalism insist that it was nearly always a ritual practice, sometimes meant as a sign of respect for the dead or as a way of absorbing magic powers, not a source of nutrition. Accusing one's enemies of cannibalism has always been a standard ploy of invaders, a way of justifying brutal treatment. A convincing case can be made that the Spanish used the idea that man-eating Caribs enslaved peaceful members of other tribes, such as the Arawaks, to justify the Spanish role in the New World slave trade.

The word *slave* derives from the root word of place-names such as Slavonia (a region of Croatia in the northern part of the former Yugoslavia), although slavery predates written history and has been documented on all continents. The Slavs were conquered by German tribes from the east in A.D. 6 and were then sold into bondage to the Romans. The Romans called them *sclavus* in medieval Latin, meaning a "Slav captive." The word entered English as *sclave* in the thirteenth century, eventually losing the *c* and coming to mean a despicable or inconsequential person, a servile or submissive follower, a servant, or a drudge.

A search for terms that a group of people actually merited yields several possibilities. Spray-painted graffiti invariably conjures up one: vandalism. The Vandals were a Germanic tribe from the Jutland Peninsula north of Germany. In the fifth century A.D., they began migrating from

95

OFF THE MAP

the Oder Valley in eastern Europe into Gaul, across the Pyrenees and into Spain, warring against the Romans and Visigoths. They developed into a maritime power and crossed into Africa, conquering Roman provinces, persecuting the Christian inhabitants, and looting sacred treasures. Vandal corsairs attacked ships in the Mediterranean and carried plundering expeditions to Sicily and southern Italy. Their sacking of Rome in 455, or the fear and hatred felt toward them by African Catholics, spawned the word *vandalism* as a term for willful or malicious destruction of property.

The pejorative adjective *byzantine* is generally used to describe policies or procedures that are complicated, inflexible, and unyielding. The term, which derives from the Byzantine Empire, also applies to social or political relationships that are devious or intricate. From 330, when Constantine I built Constantinople on the site of the ancient Greek city of Byzantium, until 1453, when the city fell to Sultan Muhammad II, invasions, violent religious controversy and schisms, political factionism, court intrigue, and social struggles prescribed a course of destruction as dramatic as the advances in learning, cartographic and otherwise, touched on earlier. Emperors competed with the Christian church. Military attacks came from all sides: Naples, Venice, Bulgaria, Serbia. The Ottoman Turks helped finish the job, encircling the empire and reducing it to Constantinople and its environs before finally extinguishing it altogether.

Albania, Greece, part of Turkey, most of the former Yugoslavia, and southeast Romania are known collectively as the Balkan states. Their political history contributed the verb *to balkanize* to the English language. It means, according to *Webster's Third New International Dictionary*, "to break up into smaller, ineffectual and frequently conflicting

96

units." The Balkans have been a nexus of European and Asian civilizations for two millennia, from ancient Greece through the Byzantine and Ottoman empires. Its population is sharply divided by ethnic, linguistic, and religious differences. The Balkan Wars of 1912–13 were emblematic of the discord now endemic to the region. Eight nations battled for the European territories of the defunct Ottoman Empire. Two combatants, Serbia and Bulgaria, were allies one year and enemies the next, each time fighting a different trio of nations. Festering tensions left in the wake of the war among most of the nations, and bitter dissatisfaction in the two countries—Bulgaria and Turkey—that had lost territory, paved the way for World War I. *Balkanized* was used as early as 1920 to describe postwar Europe generally, and the savage war in Bosnia from 1990 to 1994 seems to justify the word's original rationale.

The 1934 edition of *Webster's New International Dictionary* lists the word *ogre* as a derivative of the Byzantine *Ogor*, meaning Hungarian. Other old reference books offer the idea that the word came from the place-name Bulgaria. It was actually coined by French author Charles Perrault in 1697 as a name for a race of man-eating giants, perhaps based on the Latin *Orcus*, god of the underworld.

The word *humbug* is said to have derived from Hamburg, which gained a reputation during the nineteenth century as a prolific source of inaccurate political rumors. The city was then Germany's communication center, and "a piece of Hamburg news" became a proverbial expression for false stories. However, *humbug* had meant "hoax" or "delude" as long ago as 1750.

There's a fair amount of humbug in most of the names we've examined in this chapter. In a world where nations demand respect, the history of place-naming proves that mutual esteem is a rare commodity indeed.

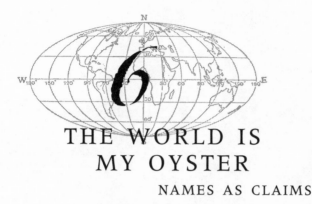

THE WORLD IS
MY OYSTER

NAMES AS CLAIMS

Redrawing the map of Africa was a primary goal of the
Berlin Conference of 1884–85, when the European countries, the United States, and the Ottoman Empire met to
expedite its colonization. The rush had already begun for
ivory, rubber, cotton, timber, gold, copper, and black con-
scripts to grow coffee and sugar. Only Liberia, on the Atlantic coast, and Ethiopia, across the continent on the Horn,
avoided being subsumed during the next thirty years. The
conference did adjust some territories, but most of the resulting agreements were too vague to last. Colonial boundaries proliferated, unrelated to geography or to the social
or political organizations of the indigenous peoples. The colonial powers created a roster of imperialism: Portuguese
Guinea, Spanish Sahara, French West Africa and German
East Africa, British Somaliland and Italian Somaliland.

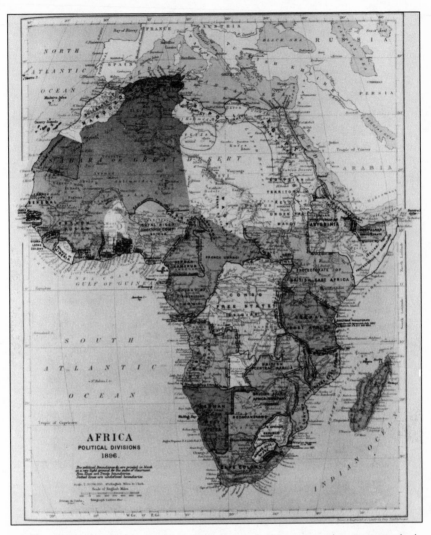

Fig. 21. *The continental land grab in Africa during the late nineteenth century attached misleading terms such as* Free State *and* Protectorate *to territories claimed by European powers. (Reproduced from the collections of the Library of Congress.)*

In the twentieth century, a certain amount of confusion attended most postcolonial name changes. Belgium had annexed the Congo Free State in 1908, making it the Belgian Congo. The country became independent in 1960 as the Congo, often called Congo-Brazzaville (at least until it changed its name to Zaire in 1971; in 1997, it became known as the Democratic Republic of the Congo) to distinguish it from its neighbor to the northwest, once part of French Equatorial Africa, independent as the Congo Republic. In 1975, Dahomey, a country in western Africa on the Gulf of Guinea, renamed itself Benin, an ancient name shown on maps of Africa dating from the mid-1600s. A minor complication with that name was the existence of a Benin City in Nigeria.

What happened in Africa had already taken place across the Atlantic in North and South America during the seventeenth and eighteenth centuries. A succession of kings in France (Louis XIV and Louis XV) and England (Charles II, William of Orange, and the Georges) vied for the lead in discovering and settling undeveloped territories, more often than not while waging war with each other. Names symbolized dominance, changing back and forth with the fortunes of war. France's Acadie became England's Nova Scotia. The French named a fort and lake after Comte de Frontenac, a colonial governor of New France, but after the French and Indian War ended and English Loyalists took over, they changed the fort's name to Kingston, and the lake's to Ontario.

The colonial feeding frenzy left a collection of place-names bestowed by nations defeated in battle. The American patriots were able to declare independence and win a revolution, casting off a potent monarchy, but the place-names remained as part of the landscape, vestiges of banished royalty. Louisiana had been named by a French

Figs. 22 and 23. *Declaring independence is only the first step toward cartographic recognition. In 1778, the nascent United States had yet to appear on this British map. Five years later, maps still mentioned the British Empire, but the United States had officially joined the list of nations. (Reproduced from the collections of the Library of Congress.)*

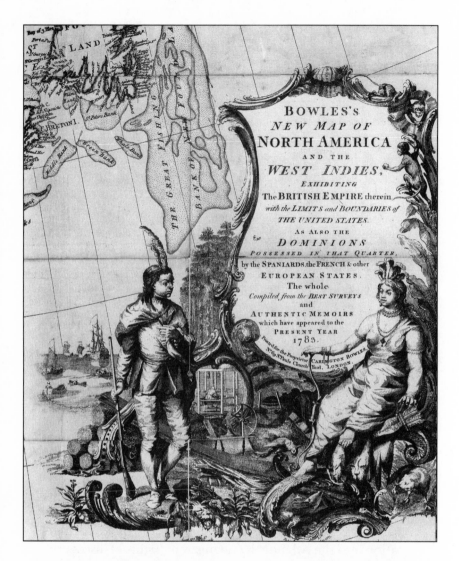

explorer in honor of Louis XIV (the name originally applied to the entire Mississippi valley). The Carolinas' names derived from the Latin version of Charles, *Carolus*, referring to England's Charles I and Charles II in the early 1600s. States were named after royal relatives (Maryland for the wife of an English king, and New York for a duke who was the brother of King Charles II) and European places (Maine after a province in France, and New Hampshire after an English county).

Free-for-all world geography reached an as-yet unrivaled height in 1493. The players were Spain and Portugal, and the referee was Pope Alexander VI, who issued a decree that fixed an imaginary north-south line of demarcation around the globe. The line passed down the Atlantic some 300 miles west of the Cape Verde Islands. To Spain he awarded the rights of discovery to all heathen lands in the unknown area west of the line (in effect, the entire New World, still unexplored); Portugal got everything in the east (namely Africa and India). The pope thus divided the non-European world between the two most powerful nations of his own continent.

Portugal was anxious to push the boundary as far west as possible. In 1494, the Treaty of Tordesillas moved it 1,200 miles beyond the Cape Verde Islands. Portugal theoretically used the revised line to claim and colonize the huge territory that is now Brazil, although controversy lingers over whether the Portuguese knew that the country existed; the Portuguese navigator Pedro Alvares Cabral didn't formally claim it until 1500, and the concept of the world as two hemispheres was not firmly established until 1512. The trade-rich Indies, halfway around the world, were a well-recognized prize. Spain agreed to the Treaty of Tordesillas because, as Portugal pushed the line of demarcation into the Atlantic, it endangered "rights of discovery" on the opposite side of the world. Both countries assigned names in South America, the Portuguese using names given by Cabral: Vera Cruz and Terra de Santa Cruz—unacceptable to the Spanish, who rightfully claimed more than half the continent, and who had made extensive explorations a year earlier than Cabral.

The treaty makers' brazen appropriation of real estate, however theoretical, heightened the importance of "accurate" cartography. The Spanish had always paid particular attention to the Indies, carefully keeping their sea charts up-to-date. The charts represented an inventory of the places they had discovered, settled, or claimed. Both countries craved the Moluccas (and the extremely valuable cargoes of spices they produced) and were determined to map these islands so that they were located in their own sphere. Portuguese cartographers placed them 43 degrees west of the line of demarcation, while the Spanish put them 3 degrees east of it, on a line passing through Sumatra. Neither nation's navigators had a method of determining longitude, and the question took years to settle. It gradually became apparent that Spain's claim was the weaker, and in 1529, Spain sold its claim to Portugal. The islands were eventually plotted at 17 degrees east, in the Portuguese sphere.

We know the Moluccas, now a province of Indonesia, as the Spice Islands, one of the most evocative names in the history of trade. The evergreen trees that bear nutmeg and cloves were native to these islands. The old meaning of "spice" also included the ingredients of incense and perfume, along with pepper, ginger, camphor, and cinnamon. Arab entrepreneurs had been first on the scene, shipping overland to the West. To ensure a monopoly, they tried to keep the location of the islands secret. Western Europeans demanded spices in order to enhance their diets and mask the odors of poorly preserved food, especially meat. When land routes were cut off by the Mongols and the Turks, European demand stimulated the search for trade routes around Africa and across the Atlantic and Pacific.

Fig. 24. *Perhaps no region on earth had as evocative a name and as huge an effect on world trade and exploration as the Spice Islands. This 1705 French map shows them as the Isles Moluques de l'Epicerie; the modern version of the name, Moluccas, is based on an old, indigenous name, Maluku. (Reproduced from the collections of the Library of Congress.)*

Consumers paid a premium either way. Adequate supplies and reliable transportation, over land or by sea, didn't reduce the cost of the condiments, because the competing nations spent fortunes trying to create and protect monopolies. Portuguese explorers and settlers arrived in Ceylon, the chief source of cinnamon, in the sixteenth century, for example, only to be displaced in the following century by the Dutch, who understandably ignored the Treaty of Tordesillas.

Prices were artificially inflated by controlled production, as in the diamond trade today. Clove trees were eliminated from all but a single island until the eighteenth century, when Arabs from Oman established massive plantations in

Zanzibar, an island in the Indian Ocean off the east coast of Africa. Although Zanzibar was then the east African center of the slave and ivory trade, the new crop earned it the nickname "Isle of Cloves."

In their heyday, the Spice Islands loomed so large in the imaginations and calculations of European mapmakers that the Catalan atlas, produced before 1375, showed more than seven thousand of them (there are actually about a thousand, with three large islands, nine island groups, and many smaller islands, not all populated) off the coast of China. The name was so familiar by the nineteenth century that it reached that ultimate mark of recognizability: it became part of a sarcastic slang term for "privy." The Spice Islands had the quintessential colonial name, one that reduced an entire culture—along with its communities, languages, religions, political structures, myths, and traditions—to a resource to be exploited. Today's "banana republic," such as Guatemala, which exports billions of pieces of fruit every year, is a modern, corporate version of places that used to earn names like Grain Coast and Tooth Coast.

The name of the ancient African kingdom of Ghana was temporarily, and accurately, transmuted to the Gold Coast. Some 500 miles north of the present-day capital of Accra, it flourished until about the eleventh century, controlling the gold trade route between mines in the south and the Saharan trade routes to the north. The Portuguese discovered it as a source of gold in 1471; it would be called the Gold Coast until 1957, when it became independent from British colonial rule and reclaimed its ancient name. It still counts gold and diamonds among its mineral resources.

As with gold, the value of copper was widely recognized in ancient times. It was one of the first metals to be mined in an organized manner, and the best source was

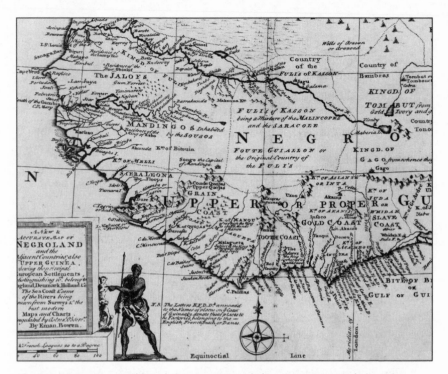

Fig. 25. Grain, ivory, gold, and slaves—as part of place-names scattered along the Guinea coast of Africa, these nouns typify the quintessential colonial name, which treats a territory as a source of riches. The names Tooth Coast and Ivory Coast were used interchangeably in the eighteenth century. (Reproduced from the collections of the Library of Congress.)

the island of Cyprus (the name probably came from the Greek word for copper, *kupros*), on the eastern end of the Mediterranean, south of Turkey. The copper deposits were so highly valued that the island saw a wave of invaders—including Egyptians, Assyrians, Phoenicians, Greeks, Persians, Romans, Syrians, Byzantines, Crusaders, French, Venetians, Turks, and English. Their combined efforts weren't sufficient to exhaust the island, however, and copper is still mined, as it is in the Andes Mountains. (One of the proposed derivations of the name Andes, incidentally, is the Peruvian *anta*, "copper.")

Another highly prized commodity was silk. The Chinese had produced it as far back as 2600 B.C. and began exporting it to Greece and Rome during the first century A.D. Greeks and Romans referred to a region in northern China, on the ancient Silk Route, as "Sarica, the fabulous Land of Silk." By keeping the manufacturing process a secret, China maintained its monopoly on raw silk until the sixth century, in part by imposing a death penalty for exporting silkworm eggs. The monopoly lasted until a pair of former missionaries to China reportedly smuggled out eggs and mulberry tree seeds to Constantinople.

When the Dutch took control of Spitsbergen (in the Arctic Ocean north of Norway) in the 1640s, they established a town called Smeerenburg (Blubberville) for salting fish and rendering blubber. Blubber drew whalers to Antarctica in the late 1800s, following in the nautical tracks of seal hunters early in the century. The 1900s saw a series of wedge-shaped, sometimes overlapping, claims to Antarctica by the United Kingdom first (in 1908), then Norway, Australia, France, New Zealand, Chile, and Argentina. International maps made in the 1920s and 1930s often reflected the claims, as do world atlases now produced by some claimants. The 1958 *Times Atlas of the World* marks the boundaries with fat red lines, showing, for example, the "Australian Antarctic Territory" and France's "Terre Adelie." American maps such as the 1993 *Hammond International World Atlas* and the 1987 *Rand McNally Cosmopolitan World Atlas* omit them, as does the 1981 *National Geographic Atlas of the World*, which includes a textual note on the 1959 Antarctic Treaty, stipulating, in part, that "no new territorial claims may be asserted." Undersea oil and mineral

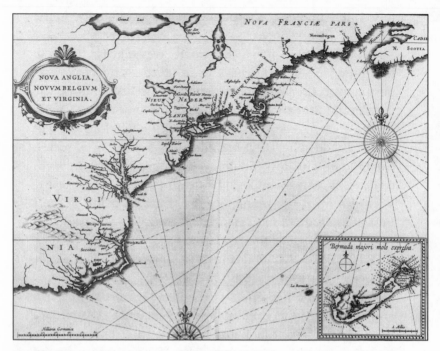

Fig. 26. *What to do with a new world? Fill it up with the same old European names, interspersed with numerous indigenous names, as on this Dutch map from 1630. (Reproduced from the collections of the Library of Congress.)*

deposits will remain untapped for the foreseeable future; in 1991, twenty-four nations signed a treaty barring exploration for fifty years.

In Africa and the Americas, if a place didn't strike colonial powers as a potential mine or plantation, it was commonplace to bring a name from home. When it gradually dawned on European explorers that they had stumbled on a new world, they wasted no time filling it up with old names. A 1639 map of North America had a Novum Belgium, Nova Francia, Nova Anglia, Nueva Biscaia, and Nueva Granada, all names that mirrored the world the explorers had left behind. Nueva Biscaia refers to the Bay of Biscay on the Atlantic coast of Europe from northwest France to northwest Spain. New Granada (formally, El Nuevo Reino de Granada) was one of the "New" places that was—at least temporarily—much bigger than the place it was named after. In fact, it included the territories now known as Colombia, Ecuador, Venezuela, and Panama. By 1830, the first three territories had split off, and in 1861, the remnants of the confederation were called the United States of New Granada. Today, the name Granada lives on in the name of Venezuela's third largest city.

Navigators and explorers from the British Isles put scores of names on the globe, from a volcanic island in the South Pacific (New Britain) to an eastern province of Canada (Nova Scotia, "Scotia" being the Latin name for Scotland). New Britain, largest of the Bismarck Archipelago and now part of Papua New Guinea, earned more than one, the first applied by British explorer William Dampier in 1700; when the island became part of German New Guinea in 1884, it was renamed Neu-Pommern (New Pomerania). James Cook named New Caledonia in 1774, using a name for Scotland that appears in poems such as Sir Walter Scott's "The Lay of the Last Minstrel" (1805):

> O Caledonia! stern and wild,
> Meet nurse for a poetic child!
> Land of brown heath and shaggy wood;
> Land of the mountain and the flood!

France annexed it in 1853, and today, as one of its overseas territories, it bears the frenchified English name Nouvel-Calédonie.

Toponymists call yet another group of externally imposed names "commemoratives," overall a fickle genre. A

Fig. 27. *Caesaria, a relic Roman name in North Africa, has long since vanished from atlases, showing the evanescence of places named after people, no matter how famous and powerful they once were. (Reproduced from the collections of the Library of Congress.)*

village in western Sardinia was called Villagio Mussolini in the early 1930s and Mussolini di Sardegna until 1944. It is now Arborea. Mussolini renamed Porto Eddo to honor his daughter; Albanian authorities changed it to Santi Quaranta. In the 1970s, cartographers for Rand McNally refused to accept Idi Amin's renaming of a lake in his own honor, figuring that the dictator's days were numbered. In the former Soviet Union, the name of the city of Naberezhnyye Chelny changed to Brezhnev in 1984, lasting just four years before the old one reappeared. Adrian Room's *Place-Name Changes Since 1900* includes thirteen towns in the Philippines, Brazil, and Cuba named after generals. How many will survive?

DEREK NELSON

Naming places after military officers or politicians is chancy, because they sometimes fall out of favor, introducing ironic overtones or forcing subsequent changes. Simon Bolivar, the Venezuelan leader in South American struggles for independence in the early 1800s, is almost unique in having had a country named for him in his lifetime. First named Alto (Upper) Peru, the nation was next called Republica Bolivar. Bolivar's brilliant military victories give him a seemingly permanent place in the pantheon of South American heroes, but his vision of an independent and united Spanish America was undermined by separatist movements. Nearly assassinated, he ended up ill and disillusioned in 1830, resigning his dictatorship-presidency after just two years in office. He died within the year.

Invasion and conquest regularly triggered renamings of places, as the new rulers put their stamp on their new possessions. Once a minor farming settlement, in the first century A.D. Rome began its expansion to an empire that stretched from the Sahara to Scotland to the Caucasus, nearly all of the known world west of Persia. The Romans left Latin place names that are still in use, including Britannia, Arabia, and Italia. Because of the Latin name Germania, English-speakers call Deutschland "Germany."

The 1917 revolution in Russia touched off the eventual renaming of perhaps half of the 700,000 towns and cities in what became the Soviet Union. Religious names or those related to the former monarchy were banished by the Communists. Joseph Stalin, the Soviet Communist leader for nearly thirty years after Lenin's death in 1924, changed his own name from Dzhugashvili to Stalin (man of steel) at age thirty-four. Grafted on to myriad places in the Soviet Union, his new name was discarded after Nikita Khrushchev and other Soviet leaders attacked the cult that had grown around his memory. Thousands of places, ranging from streets to parks to cities, had to be renamed, many for Lenin. And, continuing the pattern, Leningrad reverted to its historical name, Saint Petersburg, in 1991.

The dissolution of the USSR set off another vast cycle of renaming. Former Soviet republics adopted new English-language versions of their names—Belarus instead of Byelorussia, Kyrgyzstan rather than Kirghizia—usually restoring pre-1945 versions. The United States recently agreed to drop the *h* from Kazakstan, a reassertion of that country's own version of its name (the *h* appeared in the transliterated Russian version).

A country's urge to commemorate a hero or royalty is understandable, but the urge to commemorate oneself may be even stronger. It overtook Martin Behaim as he made his globe in Nuremberg in 1490, inserting Rio de Behemo near Cape Formoso on the Guinea Coast, and Insule Martini elsewhere. In 1472, Portuguese explorer Fernando Póo claimed an island in the Gulf of Guinea and named it after himself; Macias Nguema, who became ruler of Equatorial Guinea after it became independent in 1968, renamed the island in his own honor. He was overthrown eleven years later, and the island is now called Bioko. A current Swedish map of the world touches all the bases by labeling the island ''Macias Nguema Bioko (Fernando Póo).''

While orbiting the moon on the *Apollo 8* mission in December 1968, astronaut James Loving scanned the Sea of Tranquillity, a lava plain where the first manned landing would be made. Near the crater Secchi, an irregular mountain range winds to the south and west. Although this range had been roughly mapped from Earth, many of the individual peaks were too small to be distinguished by telescope. Lovell noticed a triangular peak, small enough to have escaped earlier identification but distinctive enough

Fig. 28. Fernando Po Island (center) was named after a Portuguese navigator (his last name is sometimes spelled Póo) who claimed it in 1472. The name stuck until a twentieth-century dictator, Macias Nguema, briefly renamed the island after himself. Nguema was quickly deposed, but the island's old name didn't return: it is now called Bioko. (Reproduced from the collections of the Library of Congress.)

to be recognized on future missions. He announced to his fellow astronauts that he was naming it after his wife; it would thereafter be called "Mount Marilyn." Who was there to say no, at least for the time being?

WHEN LANGUAGES COLLIDE

When a group of people identifies a language with a historic enemy, domestic place-names in the language are distasteful, even incendiary. If a government strips a minority group of its native tongue, as Francisco Franco did in Spain with the Catalan and Basque peoples, place-names in the new language symbolize oppression.

When the Dutch settlers known as Boers heard a radically different language in South Africa, their baffled response revealed their prejudices. Near the Cape of Good Hope, they had their first encounter with indigenous people, a tribe called the Khoikhoi (men among men). The Khoikhoi spoke one of the "click" languages, in which words are pronounced on an intake of breath and speakers use numerous tones and as many as six different types of clicking sounds. The Dutch described the Khoikhoi with the

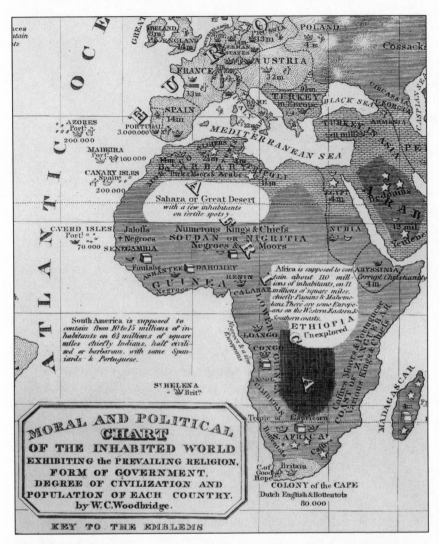

Fig. 29. At the southern tip of Africa is the land of the Hottentots, the sound of whose language was so unusual that Dutch settlers named the tribe after the Dutch words for "stammering and stuttering," hateren en tateren. (Reproduced from the collections of the Library of Congress.)

term *hateren en tateren*, "to stammer and stutter," which eventually produced the word *Hottentot*, the English name for the tribe. The *Oxford English Dictionary* lists as one meaning of the term a "person of inferior intellect or culture." This usage, which appeared in 1726, was implicit in the Boer term.

An underlying question, of course, is how earnest is the desire to comprehend. Writing in *National Geographic* magazine just after World War I, linguist Albert Guerard observed, "Language remains the worst frontier in Europe, the most complicated, the most impassable, the hardest to adjust, the most fertile in conflicts and hatred." In Western Europe, which is smaller than the United States, people speak forty languages. Four-fifths of the population speak languages belonging to three main groups: Slavic, Romance, and Germanic. Theoretically, the similarities should aid in communication. When a country is conquered or colonized, however, the indigenous language remains an integral part of ethnic identity—a "mother tongue." Danish was the language of the official and educated classes in Norway during four centuries of rule by Denmark. In the early 1800s, the growth of nationalist movements in Europe and Norway's own independence brought the drive for self-determination, a manifestation of which was the national language *nynorsk*. With its familiar and beloved words and terms, it is where place-names have their deepest roots.

To create the modern Turkish state after World War I, Mustafa Kemal replaced Arabic script with the Latin alphabet. The wearing of a fez was prohibited in 1925, just one step toward removing Islam as the state religion, accomplished three years hence. The veil, a potent symbol of female servility, was also banned, and women were given suffrage in 1934. Kemal, who would be elected president of the Turkish Republic four times, also ordered citizens to use Western-style surnames, changing his own name to Kemal Atatürk in 1934. His decrees purged Turkish of so many Persian and Arabic words that parts of old books were no longer understandable even after they had been phonetically transferred from one alphabet to another. Atatürk's actions exemplify how a country's language policies can dictate social, cultural, and political realities. Leaders of the recent Islamic revival in Turkey have tried, at times successfully, to reverse his reforms.

When Chiang Kai-shek seized Taiwan in 1949, imposing Mandarin as the national language was integral to his persecution of the Taiwanese majority. The Taiwanese referred to it as "pig language." During the mid-1980s in Bulgaria, tension between ethnic Bulgarians and Turkish Bulgarians (who make up more than 20 percent of the population) produced a government policy of mandated assimilation; nearly a million Turks were compelled to change their names to Bulgarian ones. Those who resisted were jailed or deported.

Governments new to power sometimes make a great show of preserving a local language in order to lessen agitation. In the early days of the Union of Soviet Socialist Republics, Lenin insisted that the Communists working in the administrations of the various republics should know the national languages. The Soviet government, ruling an empire that at its height enveloped people of one hundred nationalities, eventually mandated a series of national alphabets. First was a drive to romanization in the 1920s as a wedge against the Muslim heritage of certain republics. After Turkey shifted to the Roman alphabet, Stalin forced a change to Cyrillic.

With the demise of the USSR, most republics dropped Cyrillic. "Alphabet politics are at best a minor theme in

European history," Amy Schwartz observes in the October 22, 1993, issue of the *Washington Post*. "Central Asia, by contrast, seems to have functioned for long periods as a sort of Jurassic Park where the seemingly benign sciences of linguistics and phonetics run monstrously amok." The six Muslim republics in post-Soviet Central Asia are peculiarly torn between alphabets. As they cast off Cyrillic, will they choose the Roman alphabet or Arabic? Tajikistan, which is ethnically Iranian (the others are ethnically Turkic), leans toward Arabic; Kyrgyzstan, near China, opted for the Roman alphabet, and Uzbekistan probably will, too.

In July 1990, when the Ukrainian parliament declared sovereignty, a key element was passage of a law entitled "On the Languages of the Ukrainian SSR," which reinstated Ukrainian as the national and official language. For the first time in seventy years, it had regained the status of state language. Indigenous people, who make up more than two-thirds of the 52 million inhabitants, were no longer forced to speak a language that still seemed foreign.

As a child, I collected foreign coins, mostly provided by my father, who traveled around the world. Some of the coins he brought back were more "foreign" than others. Many names written in the Roman alphabet were intelligible to me: Türkiye, Jugoslavija, Polska, Nederland, España. Coins from Norge, Eire (decorated with a whale and a harp), and Island (the Icelandic spelling of Iceland) confused me. The source of a tiny aluminum coin bearing a stylized rampant lion and the legend "Česka Republika" was another puzzle, as was a bronze-colored coin whose cryptic legend appeared to say "Elliniki," in Greek. Japanese coins offered no clues, then or now.

This old coin collection sketches the diversity of the

world's tongues and alphabets. There are more than six thousand registered languages (not counting dialects), an average of nearly thirty per sovereign state. The Solomon Islands, with a population of 350,000, has ninety local languages. People in Papua New Guinea speak languages and dialects from seven hundred linguistic groups; most of these languages are mutually unintelligible. Many nations have two or more official languages, each with different purposes. In Kenya, English is the official and international language, while Kiswahili is the national and cultural language. Radio stations broadcast in those two and sixteen other languages.

One-third of the thirty-three-letter Cyrillic alphabet does not correspond to single letters in English. The Cambodian language has seventy-two letters, the highest number used in an alphabetic language. In Sri Lanka, the Tamil language uses 12 symbols for vowels and diphthongs, 18 for consonants, and 187 combinations and ligatures to create syllables. Arabic and Hebrew vowels must, in general usage, be inferred from context.

The fundamental differences between the world's most common language (Mandarin) and second most common language (English, which is spoken by about half as many people) illustrate the difficulties of trying to represent corresponding sounds. English is made up of letters that represent sounds and that can be rearranged to spell words. Written Mandarin is based on seventeen brush strokes that represent simple words or ideas instead of sounds, with thousands of combinations. Unlike English, spoken Mandarin is a tonal language. English words such as *tear* or *row* have different meanings and/or pronunciations in different contexts, but they look identical.

In spite of such technical problems, names must migrate between languages. Those made up of common nouns un-

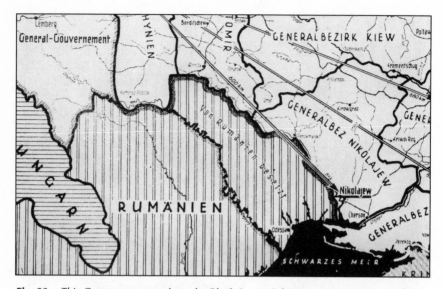

Fig. 30. *This German map translates the Black Sea as Schwarzes Meer. Ungarn is the German version of Hungary's name. (Reproduced from the collections of the Library of Congress.)*

dergo simple translation. What English speakers call the Black Sea is Schwarzes Meer in German. New York appears as Nueva York on a Brazilian world map. On Swedish maps, the Ivory Coast is Elfenbens Kusten and Tierra del Fuego is Eldslandet. Portuguese maps show the former as Costa do Marfim, the Red Sea as Mar Vermelho, and Newfoundland as Terra Nova. West Virginia in Spanish is Virginia Occidental.

The usual method of transferring names between languages that use different signifiers is transliteration, transforming spellings from the letters of one alphabet to the closest corresponding letters of another. When a nonalphabetic language, such as Chinese or Japanese, is brought into English by transcribing from spoken words, it is said to be romanized.

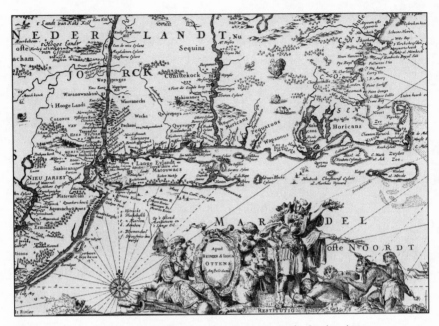

Fig. 31. *The Dutch West India Company founded New Netherland and New Amsterdam in the 1620s. Forty years later, under England's King Charles II, these places became the colonies of New York and New Jersey. The way this seventeenth-century Dutch map spells Nieuw Jorck and Lange Eylandt (Long Island), however, hints at the Dutch origins. (Reproduced from the collections of the Library of Congress.)*

An internationally accepted Roman alphabet has proven elusive for several reasons. The languages that use forms of this alphabet assign different values to consonants such as *c*, *g*, *j*, *v*, and *w*. Greek, Persian, Russian, and Turkish use many consonants that lack precise equivalents in the Roman alphabet; they also use comparatively few vowels (whereas in English, four of the five most common letters are vowels). The uvular *r* sound in French and the trilled *r* sound in Spanish have subtle values that cannot be rendered by a single, unadorned letter.

Linguists have not developed a universally accepted way to transliterate Arabic, either. One of the largest collections

DEREK NELSON

Fig. 32. When a place-name includes nouns, translation is one of the easiest ways for mapmakers who speak different languages to transfer names between cultures if they want to. Tierra del Fuego, Spanish for "land of fire," becomes Terre de Feu for the French but remains Terra del Fuego for the English. The Cape of Good Hope is Cabo da Boa Esperança in its original language, Portuguese. (Reproduced from the collections of the Library of Congress.)

of Arabic maps was published in Konrad Miller's *Mappae Arabicae* between 1926 and 1931. Miller was particularly interested in identifying place-names, but many of his identifications were wrong because his transliterations were faulty. Furthermore, Arabic does not distinguish between upper-case and lower-case letters, and the Latin letters chosen to represent various phonetic sounds vary (as does spelling), depending upon the translator. For example, Arabic includes characters called the *hamza* and the *ayn*, which are pronounced by expelling air. The former corresponds to the Greek "smooth breathing" (as the vowel sound of *in*), the latter to the Greek "rough breathing" (as in the vowel sound of *hen*). The *hamzah* is sometimes represented by an apostrophe, which presents an obvious problem since English uses that mark to indicate possessives and dropped letters in contractions.

Given such stumbling blocks to accuracy and consistency, and considering the world's relative unwillingness to adapt to linguistic changes, it surprised many when, during the 1950s, the Chinese substituted a new system of romanizing Mandarin for a once widely accepted system. The Wade-Giles system was developed by Sir Thomas Wade, a British diplomat and China scholar who became Cambridge University's first professor of Chinese. He published its rudiments in 1859. In 1912, Herbert Giles, another Cambridge professor, improved it and added a dictionary. Wade-Giles was standard until the Chinese government introduced Pinyin. Based on the Peking dialect of Mandarin, which it was meant to establish as national, Pinyin would in turn standardize pronunciations among Chinese minorities.

One of the problems with Wade-Giles was that it had been based on the pronunciation of nonstandardized speech sounds. Pinyin rendered pronunciation more precisely, dispensed with hyphens, and simplified spellings. The *ch* in a name like Chou, rendered as such in the Wade-Giles system, became *zh* in Pinyin. Most usages of the letter *k* changed to *g*, and *p* became *b*. Wade-Giles rendered the name of China's capital Pei-ching or Pei-p'ing; the Pinyin version is the now familiar Beijing. In fact, the name has been spelled at least five ways in English during the twentieth century. Peking, "northern capital" in Mandarin, may still be the most familiar version for older readers. In 1928, when Chiang Kai-shek established his government in Nan-

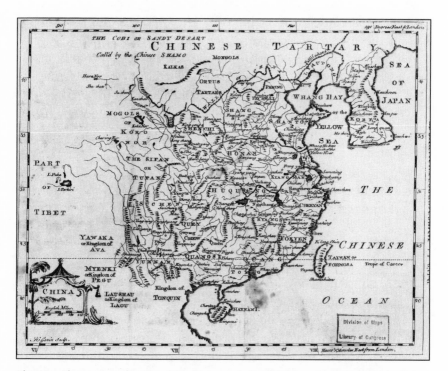

Fig. 33. *The process of writing Chinese names in English was not standardized until the nineteenth century. This 1767 map shows typical loosely phonetic versions: Fokyen (formerly Fukien, now Fujian), Honan (Hunan), and Taywan. (Reproduced from the collections of the Library of Congress.)*

jing, the "southern capital," the name changed to Pei-p'ing (also written Peiping, and sometimes spelled with an initial *B*), meaning "northern peace." Chiang's government had received foreign recognition after the military victory of his Kuomintang over the Communists. After the Chinese People's Republic was established in 1949, however, the old name of Peking was officially revived, although American diplomats and journalists continued to call it Peiping for a number of years. Then came the transliteration Beijing, a spelling that finally seems to have established itself in our national consciousness, but only after decades of repetition in the media (which converted reluctantly), academic acceptance (similarly long in coming), and official recognition by the Board on Geographic Names. China's growing role as a world economic power has helped cement the change. Since 1979, the Chinese government has mandated Pinyin for all translated diplomatic and foreign-language publications.

Linguists have long known that people find it hard to discern exact values of unfamiliar sounds. Even after the ear is trained, reproducing them can be difficult. The orthographic way to show various sounds is with diacritical marks, but reference books tend to omit them because editors find that they clutter the text and confuse readers. Yet, assuming the goal is something more than a pidgin-English misspelling that would seem ludicrous to a native speaker of the language being reproduced, they are important. Their absence is one factor among many contributing to transcultural linguistic decay.

Domestic phonetic decay, "by which the words of a nation's speech are clipped and worn down by constant currency," was described by the Reverend Isaac Taylor: "Like ancient coins, the legend which they bore at first has become effaced." The decay may start subtly, a letter here and there. Andalusia, a region in southern Spain, was Vandalusia, named for the Vandals, who invaded it circa A.D. 400. In February 1995, New Mexico's state legislature asked Albuquerque's city council to restore an *r* that somehow fell out of the name of the Duke of Alburquerque, one-time viceroy of New Spain, for whom the city was named in 1706.

In the early 1900s, pro-Spanish enthusiasts campaigned to standardize the correct Spanish pronunciation of Los Angeles, "lohs ang' hay lez." The city's Spanish heritage was clear in its original name, Nuestra Señora Reina de los Angeles, which dates from the Spanish founding of the city in 1781. California was sufficiently bilingual to handle the old pronunciation, but the idea fizzled. Perhaps the melting pot had been bubbling too long, or the Spanish pronunciation seemed un-American to the citizens who held most of the political power. Politicians referred to "the City of Angels" until the controversy died down.

Sometimes the English mispronunciation of a local name can be traced to a distinct source. During the Middle Ages, Crusaders brought the name Cairo not from the Saracens, who correctly pronounced it "al-ka'-he-ro," but from the Venetians and the Genoese. Our current pronunciation of Copenhagen is not from the Danish but the German form, which we can pronounce more easily, though still imperfectly.

Fiji's true name was Viti, but the neighboring Tonga islanders mispronounced it. European missionaries in the Tongas perpetuated that pronunciation, and multiple spellings persisted through the nineteenth century. The 1874 edition of *The Imperial Gazetteer* lists Fiji, Feejee, Fidji, and Viti. The original Sinhalese name of Colombo, capital of Sri Lanka, was Kalantotta. It was on the Kelani River, and the name meant "Kelani ferry." Arab traders gradually corrupted the name to Kolambu. The Portuguese in turn rendered it Colombo.

Mispronunciation's twin is misunderstanding, which has produced several well-known place-names. When foreign traders asked the Chinese about their place of origin, they apparently answered with the name of the ruling dynasty (the Tsin or Chin, 420–265 B.C.) instead of the name of their country, Kung-ho-kuo. The name of the dynasty was then latinized by the Romans as *Sina*, a form that

129

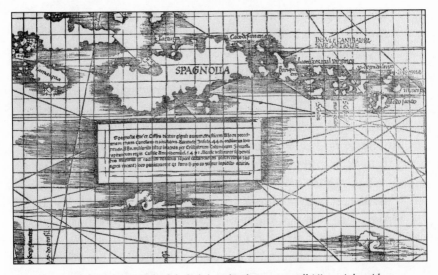

Fig. 34. *Medieval maps usually labeled the island we now call Hispaniola with variations on older spellings. The Spanish* Española *was often rendered "Spagnola." Over centuries, the spelling (and resulting pronunciation) of such names often underwent subtle changes. The double l in the name is unusual, but consistent orthography was not a hallmark of medieval maps, which were often copied by people who couldn't read or write. (Reproduced from the collections of the Library of Congress.)*

should have led to an English version that started with an *s* sound. However, contact with the Malays, who controlled trade with the Chinese, brought their pronunciation, which began with a *ch*, into European usage.

Countless similar spelling variations abound throughout history. In a Catalan atlas published in 1375, Guinea appears as "Ginuia," and the town of Tenbuch (Tombouctou) lies along the route from Morocco to the Niger River. A state on a map of New England drawn in the early to mid-1700s is labeled "Konektikut." On one of Cook's 1769 charts of the South Pacific, Tahiti is spelled "Otahette."

Our modern, Webster-esque notion is that a single, "correct" spelling exists. In fact, the spelling of Jamaica, for example, wasn't standardized until well after English settlers arrived in 1655. Although Columbus had tried to rename the island, it reverted to an Arawak Indian name that the Spaniards wrote as Xaymaca. In letters and journals, Englishmen spelled it Gemecoe, Gemegoe, Jamico, Jammaca, and Jamecah.

Current American usage is a profoundly mixed bag. Occasionally, we use the name that local people use, even pronouncing it correctly: Afghanistan, Bangladesh, Zambia, and Zimbabwe pose little problem. Some pronunciations are tricky. Belarus doesn't rhyme with "Polaris"; there is no "cube" in the Spanish pronunciation of Cuba and no "hate" in the French pronunciation of Haiti. For the record, the correct ways to say these names are "bell-uh-roose'," "koo'va" or "koo'ba," and "a-ee'tee'." The Spanish pronunciation of Argentina is "ar-khayn-tee'na," and Chile sounds like "chee'lay." In Portuguese, Moçambique is pronounced "moo'sem-be'ke."

Kriesnadath Nandoe, UN ambassador at the Permanent Mission of Suriname, says, "Americans do not pronounce the country's name correctly. It has to be pronounced 'sureenaamo.' " Turkey is properly pronounced "tuerkeeye." In Hawaii, pronunciation of the state's name marks speakers as locals or *haoles*, interlopers. The former say "ha-va'-ee," the latter "he-wa'yee."

Transliterations of Arabic names can reveal the sounds from which the more familiar English version derived: Algeria from Al-Jazairiya; Comoros from Al-Qumur; Jordan from Al-Urduniya. The process works in both directions. On English-language maps made by Arab nations, Alexandria appears as Al-Iskandarīyah. The commemoration of Alexander the Great, who founded the city in 332 B.C., is neatly submerged in an Arabic-sounding name.

Bilingual dictionaries and maps from other countries reveal the helter-skelter manner in which names move between languages. Usage is maddeningly illogical. A Swedish world map shows the Gulf of Alaska and Mexikanska Golfen, New Mexico and Nya Guinea. A Portuguese map of the world partly translates one American name (Nova Orleans) and alters the spelling of others, such as Filadelfia. Kenya appears as Quênia. A couple of names are much closer to the medieval versions than modern English versions: Calcutta is Calecute (Vasco da Gama rendered it Kalikut in the early 1500s), and the Caribbean Sea is Mar do Caribe.

Japanese-English dictionaries provide more examples. For some countries, Japanese syllables happen to match: Uganda, San Marino, Togo, Dominica. Other names get translated. The Arctic Ocean is Hoppyoyo, "northern ice sea"; the Dead Sea is Shikai. Greenland appears as both Ryokuto, "green island," and Gurinrando, a phonetic version of the English name. Phonetic versions were easy for some countries, such as France (Furansu), and tortuous for others, such as Newfoundland (Nyufuaundorando) and Liechtenstein (Rihitenshiyutain). The phonetic versions of some names derive from the English version of their names: Holland is Oranda instead of an adaptation of the Dutch version, Nederland. Others derive from the country's own language: Germany is Doitsu (from Deutschland), and Belgium is Berugi (from the Flemish België). Japanese characters reading Kan-bo-ji-a precede the English-language name Khmer Republic (the 1970–75 name of Democratic Kampuchea, formerly Cambodia).

A German-English dictionary also translates some names and transliterates others. Tierra del Fuego is Feuerland, "fire land," and the Rocky Mountains are das Felsengebirge (*felsen* means "rock," "crag," or "cliff," and *gebirge* means "mountain range"). The Baltic Sea appears as der

Ostsee, "eastern sea" (it is northeast of Germany), and die Fidschi-Inseln is the Fiji Islands. Madagasse is the Malagasy Republic, the pre-1975 name of Madagascar, based on the island's precolonial name, adopted after independence from France.

If linguists and cartographers could create a global language, assuming it rendered names in a neutral manner, an acceptable international map would be within reach. Latin fit the bill during the Renaissance in Europe, serving as the language of scholars and writers. European diplomats used it until the seventeenth century, and it was widely used in academic writing in the nineteenth century. But Latin was more a continental than a global language, of little use in the Arab world and the Orient. The conditions that made it so useful in Europe—small political units that had diverse cultures and that strongly resisted unification—certainly exist around the world today, but Latin isn't poised for a comeback. The centers of global economic power are too widely dispersed and too diverse. The United Nations makes do with five official languages: Chinese, English, French, Russian, and Spanish.

English is the world's most common second language, and the international language of business and computers. Perhaps the Internet, on which English predominates, will gradually establish it as the world's lingua franca. As a neutral global language, Esperanto, more of a linguistic curiosity than a feasible alternative, has been giving it the old college try for most of the twentieth century. When Americans, a pragmatic and hardly tradition-bound people, refuse to adopt something as logical as the metric system, the idea of all cultures accepting a new and different language seems quixotic.

Nine of the world's major powers did try to cooperate

133

on a map once: the great International Map of the World. It took four annual conferences just to set the ground rules. The original proposal came from a young Viennese geography professor, Albrecht Penck, in 1891; the project was formally launched at the Ninth International Geographical Congress in Geneva in 1908. Its 2,500 maps would be unbiased and inclusive, able to be read and interpreted by people from almost every nation. The British government invited Austria-Hungary, France, Germany, Italy, Japan, Russia, Spain, and the United States to send delegates to a conference in London in 1909; everyone except Japan attended. The map would use the local form of each name, the way it appeared on each country's own official maps (Florence, for instance, would be Firenze). Each country would be responsible for its own national survey (some undeveloped countries had never had one and weren't equipped to do one). Map text was to be written in the language of the country that published the map, plus one of the three official languages (English, French, and German), using the Roman alphabet, accompanied by explanations of phonetic values. The spelling of place-names in countries that used the Roman alphabet would "follow authorized custom," a nebulous concept made even less meaningful by the huge number of European colonies and possessions scattered around the globe, for which the authorized names would presumably not be authorized by the native people.

Organizers noted, "It is desirable that European and other governments which do not use the Latin alphabet should publish in Latin characters, an authorized system of transliteration." When a place had "a distinctly different name in common use," that name would be shown in smaller type. Geographic features that extended into more than one country would have the name in both languages.

Work formally began at a conference in Paris in 1913; nearly three dozen countries joined the effort. The Central Bureau of the Map of the World was established at the Ordnance Survey, a British mapping agency in Southampton, England. The question of how to spell place-names turned out be a minor problem compared to the disaster that loomed ahead: World War I. By then, the original plan had been cut by more than a third, and only eight maps had been published. The project was resumed after the war, and by 1921, most of the original participants were back at work. The next twenty years saw steady progress. By the end of the 1930s, 405 maps had been published, but only about half conformed to the original pattern. World War II derailed the project again when the German air force bombed the Central Bureau at Southampton, turning most of its map collection and archives into charred confetti.

The International Map of the World was about half done when the United Nations took over the project in 1953. According to Miklos Pinther, chief of the UN cartographic section, they stopped issuing reports about ten years ago because of a general lack of international interest. He estimates that some 800 maps, covering most of the land areas, were published. The eighty-year saga of the International Map of the World dramatizes what happens when an ambitious and laudable idea collides with recalcitrant reality.

MULTIPLE NAMES
MEAN CONFUSION AND
CONTENTION

Place-names would not offer such fertile ground for research if the use of multiple names for a single place had an obvious explanation. Centuries of national custom dictate our choice of names for other countries. Some names have been used in English for so long that it is expedient to continue using them, even after they have been discarded by the countries they refer to. We know these names and can pronounce them. English speakers recognize the body of water between England and Europe as the English Channel. But calling it "English" implies ownership. To avoid symbolically ceding the channel to their ancient rivals on the other side, the French call it La Manche, "the sleeve." Japanese mapmakers compromise with Ei-futsu Kaikyo, "English-French Channel."

Koreans aren't happy about the name of the Sea of Ja-

Fig. 35. *Korean diplomats and cartographers are currently engaged in an international campaign to establish the name East Sea as a valid alternative to the name Sea of Japan. This 1705 map shows that the body of water was also called Sea of Korea. If a place-name implies ownership (such as in the name English Channel), there's likely to be a neighboring country that resents and denies it. (Reproduced from the collections of the Library of Congress.)*

pan, either, and have embarked on an international campaign to undermine its validity. The name Sea of Korea appeared on numerous maps in the seventeenth and eighteenth centuries. Korean scholars trace the spread of the name Sea of Japan to Japanese expansionism in the late nineteenth century. The Korean name is Tong Hae, "east sea," which appears in the national anthem. Korean diplomats have suggested that world cartographers use both names.

Postage stamps from Argentina label the Falklands as the Islas Malvinas, signifying the prevailing view that the British occupation of the islands is illegitimate. A staff member in the map room at the Library of Congress recalls that, during the short, undeclared Falkland Islands War in 1982, visitors from England and Argentina objected to staff usage of the "wrong" name. Similar scenes, in a hundred contexts, occurred after both world wars.

Where do all these conflicting names come from? To start with, modern nations have official names, established by government decree, internal law, or a country's constitution. Many countries have also acquired unofficial names and often have familiar historic names. Conquest and colonialism filled gazetteers with additional names, as did newly independent countries that adopted new names or retrieved old ones.

Country names are usually spelled differently in various languages, which multiplies the options. Some names can be translated easily: the United States becomes Estados Unidos or États-Unis. Many countries have more than one official language, which gives them multiple names. Switzerland has four: Suisse (French), Schweiz (German), Svizzera (Italian), and Svizra (Romansh). In Latin, its name was Helvetia. The English version is most like German; it comes from the canton Schwyz, one of the original three to align

Figs. 36 and 37. *Is the correct name Falkland Islands or Islas Malvinas? The Spanish map is from 1799, thirty-three years before Great Britain occupied the islands. The British map is from 1856. Some modern postage stamps from Argentina show the old name, as national leaders dispute the legitimacy of England's claim. National maps sometimes depict what national leaders wish were true. (Reproduced from the collections of the Library of Congress.)*

DEREK NELSON

in 1291. The name also appears in the name of the language spoken by 65 percent of the population of Switzerland, a German dialect called *Schwyzerdütsch*.

For rivers and mountains that span nations, it is simply convenient to use one name. The Danube River collects a handful of names in the languages of the countries it flows through—and Danube is not among them.

Fig. 38. *Why don't we call some countries by the names they call themselves? This 1529 map shows at least two Latin-based English variants: Germania (instead of the native Deutschland) and Hungaria (source of the name Hungary for the country that calls itself Magyarország). (Reproduced from the collections of the Library of Congress.)*

During the past fifty years, editors and authors have tried various strategies aimed at standardizing usage of place-names, but the practical and pragmatic often butt heads. Adopting "authentic" names (those in use by local people) has long been a widely recognized goal of international cartographic groups and influential publications. In 1899, when the Seventh International Geographical Congress met in Berlin, representatives decided that native names should prevail over others, a principle supported during the next few years by the Royal Geographic Society, the Colonial Division of the German Foreign Office, and the United States Geographic Board (as it was then called).

The rapid spread of World War II across the globe pro-

DEREK NELSON

duced a stylistic crisis for American press agencies and newspapers, which scrambled to standardize the spelling of the place-names that reporters used when describing battles. Citing the "varied and haphazard" spelling that made places hard to identify, an article in the July 1944 issue of *National Geographic* noted, "Thousands of places lead double lives in the atlas. Many cities and other places in European news recently have been spelled two ways, and one spelling gives little clue to the other." Examples included Bratislava, a city in the south central region of the former Czechoslovakia, called Pressburg by the Germans from 1939 to 1945; Cheb, in western Czechoslovakia, called Eger before 1918 and from 1939 to 1945 by the Germans; and Sopron in western Hungary, which the Germans called Ödenburg prior to 1921. The names of certain Russian towns had been spelled four different ways in different papers on the same day, and some newspapers didn't spell names consistently two days in a row.

In 1985, the United Nations adopted the spelling Côte d'Ivoire, based on that country's official policy. *The World Almanac* now lists Côte d'Ivoire as the primary spelling, but many publications in the United States continue with the older English version. In the preface to *Place-Names of the World*, Adrian Room notes "an increasing tendency for place-names in present-day atlases, encyclopedias and reference works to be given in their native version or spelling." He doesn't follow that trend, however, noting that "where a place is known by two equally acceptable names—even if one is now historically inappropriate—I have given both." He mentions Siam and Thailand as an example; as we will see, the phrase "equally acceptable" refers primarily to English-language readers.

Modern scholars often view place-names against the backdrop of colonialism. In his 1988 *Historical Dictionary of*

Zaire, F. Scott Bobb notes, "Although international cartographers generally prefer the name 'Congo River' to describe Zaire's major river, I have used the official Zairian name, 'Zaire River.' Likewise I have used Lake Edouard to describe the eastern lake that for a time was called Lake Idi Amin but was changed by Ugandan authorities following the demise of the Amin government."

Today, the Board on Geographical Names, in liaison with international groups such as the United Nations, permits the use of conventional names that have become established in English, even though they differ from local official names: Munich (München), Cologne (Köln), Vienna (Wien), Venice (Venezia). According to Miklos Pinther at the UN Department of Public Information, "Toponymy on our maps tends to reflect native, local usage except where widely accepted conventional forms exist. Hence, we would not use, for example, Mişr for Egypt" on English-language maps. Nor does the government of Egypt seem particularly interested in changing the international usage of its name to the Arabic form: "When people want to see the pyramids, they think of the name Egypt, not Mişr," notes Dr. Michael Dobson, the chief cartographer for the Rand McNally Publishing Group.

The name Mişr does appear on a map of the Middle East made by Baedeker, a German company famous for its guidebooks. Maps printed in Europe or the Middle East for domestic use contain other names that seem unconventional to Americans. On the Baedeker map, for example, India is Bharat, the Red Sea is Bhar Al-Ahmaar, and Cairo is Al-Qāhirah. The Shell Eurokarte series, published in Germany, also uses local names (Luxembourg is called Grand-Duche Grossherzogtum). Borders often list dual names; a German-Hungarian map entitled Polen-Polska shows cities labeled in both languages: Pozen-Poznan, Warschau-

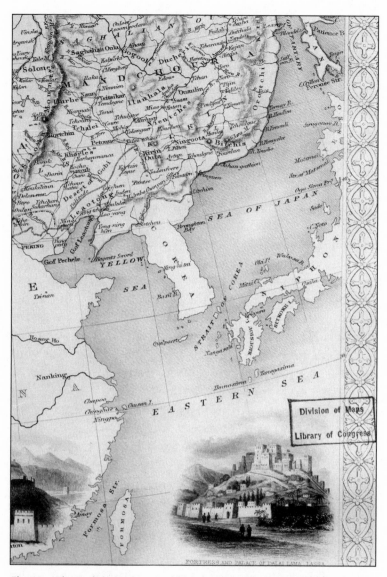

Fig. 39. The English-speaking world has used the name Japan for centuries. A few maps—including this 1851 map of eastern Asia—show the native version of the name, here with an older spelling. (Reproduced from the collections of the Library of Congress.)

Warszawa, and Breslau-Wrocław. A 1993 map of Hungary, printed in Budapest, shows the country's name in three languages on the cover: Ungarn (German), Hongrie (French), and Magyarország (Hungarian). One evening in August 1995, "Shqipëri" was a $500 answer (the hardest level) on the television quiz show *Jeopardy!* The question was, "What is Albania?"

Selecting place-names is a regular issue for the staff at the National Geographic Society, a prolific publisher of maps, atlases, and articles about the world's nations. According to Juan José Valdés, assistant director of cartography, "There are no hard and fast rules when it comes to deciding which place-names to use on our maps. However, we do analyze the names and their various forms before we make a final selection. We not only try to determine if the name is recognized by the geographic and cartographic community, but we also investigate if the place-name is used in the country in question. Sometimes some of our members question the legitimacy of our selection, as with our use of Macedonia and our recognition of Tibet as being part of China."

A letter from a Spanish reader, which appeared in the November 1991 issue of *National Geographic,* illustrates Valdés's point: "Your cartographer labeled Dongbei as Manchuria. I traveled that area in 1976 and at that time, at least, to have referred to it as Manchuria would have been to lower the ambient temperature well below freezing."

The editor replied, "Manchuria, which has imperialistic overtones to many Chinese, is the region's historic name. Dongbei, an unofficial name, means 'northeast' and refers to the three northeastern provinces." The Manchus, who conquered China from the north in the seventeenth century and ruled until the twentieth, tried to keep Manchuria

146

DEREK NELSON

as a Manchu preserve, limiting Chinese immigration, but were eventually absorbed by the general population.

Valdés points out that the *National Geographic* style doesn't always coincide with that of the Board on Geographic Names. In Egypt and Israel, the BGN sometimes uses an older British system of spelling. *National Geographic* uses the spellings on the national surveys of those countries. For Rand McNally's map editors, as is the case with their counterparts at the National Geographic Society, questions about forms of place-names come up incessantly. Distributing maps internationally, Rand McNally works to reflect world usage and makes extensive use of both proper names and alternate names. The company's maps now reflect the change from Ivory Coast to Côte d'Ivoire, for example, which BGN approved several years ago.

A *New York Times* editorial on September 20, 1987, raised the issue of what to call the Persian Gulf. The writer called it "a body of water nearly surrounded by Arabians who hate the name" and who call it the Arabian Gulf. British newspapers and the BBC called it "the Gulf." The writer suggested, as a neutral alternative, the original name for the Persian Gulf, A-ab-ba, "great water," which was what the Sumerians called it 5,000 years ago. Barring that, how about the Sumerian Gulf?

Another recent place-name controversy involves Burma, which has been racked with internal dissension and insurgency since 1948. Three political events of the previous year—the assassination of General Aung San (the country's popular leader), the ascent to leadership of his successor, and independence—led the Karen, one of four populous ethnic minorities, to pit themselves against government troops in battle, demanding a nation separate from the Burmese majority. Other minority groups fol-

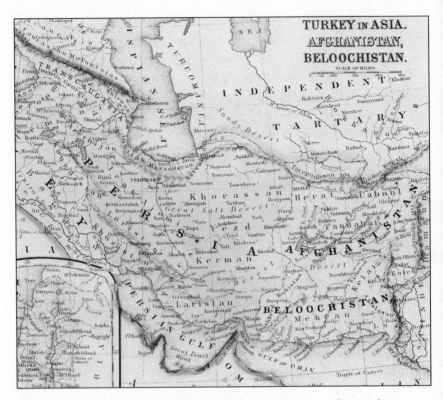

Fig. 40. You can buy a Persian cat and a Persian rug, but you can't buy a ticket to Persia, and you can't find it on the map anymore. When the original place-name changes, some peculiar memorials remain. (Reproduced from the collections of the Library of Congress.)

lowed suit. From 1962 to 1988, the country was ruled by a dictator and endured a scale of violence almost unsurpassed in the rest of the world, with hundreds of demonstrators for democracy killed and thousands pushed across the border with Thailand. In 1989, military leaders of the junta now in place announced the change of name to Myanmar, ostensibly to reflect ethnic diversity, though in fact Myanmar derives from the majority Burmese version of the country's name (Pyeitawinzu Myanma Naingngandaw). The junta leaders also decreed that all English-language signs in the capital city that used to say "Rangoon" now must read "Yangon." The former names, they decided, were reminders of British colonialism. Burma had gone to war with Great Britain in 1824 because of friction on the border with India, and in 1886, England triggered another war to preempt growing French strength in the area, ruling Burma as a colony until 1947.

The new name has been slow to catch on. Undoubtedly, our national reluctance to adopt it is due in part to the fact that the repressive military junta in Burma-Myanmar is among the world's worst abusers of the human rights of its citizens. The military government declared a May 1990 election invalid and detained the leaders of the victorious party, including General Aung San's daughter, Aung San Suu Kyi, who was under house arrest when she won the Nobel Peace Prize in 1991.

In June 1995, *Newsweek*, calling the country a "dystopian Shangri-la," used the name Burma and pointed out that it "now calls itself Myanmar." A photo caption in the May 1995 issue of *National Geographic* mentions the "rugged border passes between Myanmar and Thailand." *The World Almanac* lists "Burma (see Myanmar)." Correspondents on National Public Radio still say Burma. The Board on Geographic Names has not yet approved the change.

After the American withdrawal from Vietnam, the new Vietnamese government gave Saigon a new name: Ho Chi Minh City. Saigon (sandy shore or west river) was an adequate name, taken from the river on whose estuary the city is located. Unfortunately, Saigon had also been the enemy's capital, so the new regime installed the name of its extremely popular wartime leader, Ho Chi Minh, president of North Vietnam from 1954 until 1969. He had lived in the United States during World War I, later helped found the French Communist Party, and organized the Vietnamese independence movement after World War II. The 1954 Geneva Conference that split the country provided for elections to be held two years later, aimed at reuniting the country, but South Vietnam (with the backing of the United States) refused, perhaps fearing that Ho's popularity would reunite the country under Communist rule. When *National Geographic* ran an article about the city in April 1995, editors entitled it "The New Saigon," adding the subhead "Now officially Ho Chi Minh City." City officials, it noted, still refer to the city as Saigon—more evidence that "official" and "actual" are two different things.

For purposes other than maps, the United Nations accepts the name that a country establishes as its official version. Member nations also have the right to recommend foreign-language versions of their own names, a policy that has its detractors. English geographical names are often misunderstood, argued Marcel Aurousseau in *The Rendering of Geographical Names*:

> In June, 1939, the Siamese Government announced by official decree that the name of Siam would thenceforth be Thailand "in the English language." Unfortunately, British authorities acquiesced in the change, and the bastard name Thailand has gained currency as a postal name. But that we should renounce our living name "Siam" in favour of one which the Siamese themselves do not use (they call their country Prathet Thai or Muang Thai) is, I hope, unlikely while English is a living tongue. . . . It was no more appropriate for the Siamese to decide what their country is to be called in our language than it

would be for us to decide what anything is to be called in Siamese.

Aurousseau's position is hard to defend. Names and self-determination are intimately entwined. If, before the American Revolution, England had formally referred to the United States as the North American Colonies, and then continued to call it that after losing the war, would Patrick Henry have shrugged his shoulders? In the case of the former Siam, a bloodless coup deposed the monarchy in 1932. Six years later, one of the leaders of the coup, Pibul Songgram, became premier and changed the country's name to Thailand. What happened to the name during the next decade dramatizes the symbolic value of place-names. In 1942, Songgram allied with the Japanese and declared war on the United States and England. A second leader of the 1932 coup, Pridi Phanomyang, formed a militant antigovernment underground and became premier in the postwar government. He promptly jailed Pibul as a war criminal and restored the name Siam, publicly repudiating Pibul's policies. In 1947, Pibul led an overthrow of Pridi's government and back came the name Thailand. The fact that Siam perhaps derived from the Sanskrit *sian*, meaning "brown" (in reference to the skin color of the natives), suggests another distasteful aspect of the name.

Dr. Meredith Burrill, executive secretary of the Board on Geographic Names, wrote in 1958:

People all over the world now have occasion to refer to, identify, or even go to places that their ancestors either never heard of or considered so far away and inaccessible as to be of no concern. It has become increasingly evident that the old process of bending names from other sound systems into written forms compatible with the systems of the receiver language, producing what we call "conventional" names, was consistent with the ideas, attitudes and limited geographical needs of earlier times. That process is inconsistent with today's concepts of international cooperation and of respect for people who speak other languages, and inconsistent with the enormously greater number of geographic names with which people must deal.

Inconsistency, unfortunately, seems to be an unavoidable feature of international usage.

In the 1980s, Canadian provinces, notably the Northwest Territories and Quebec, began to adapt official maps to local usage by substituting indigenous names for those imposed by European explorers. Cree, Inuit, and other native names are finding their way onto the globe, reflecting gains in political power. As a mark of increased autonomy, the Spanish government has allowed the Basque provinces of Asturias, Galicia, Catalonia, and Valencia to change place-names from Castilian to native forms. In America, there are thousands of Native American names extant, and the Board on Geographic Names encourages use of or reversion to those "linguistically appropriate to the area."

When Greenland, a Danish colony, got home rule in May 1979, its indigenous citizens promptly began using Inuit names for their country (Kalâtdlit Nunât, "the land of man") and their capital, the country's oldest Danish colony, founded in 1721. It had been Godthåb (good hope) and became Nuuk (small cape). A recent American map shows the capital's new name, with Godthåb in parentheses. A new Swiss map in English makes the new country name primary, with the name Greenland in parentheses.

When France recognized Algeria's sovereignty in 1962,

Guyotville became Ain Benian, and Duperre became Ain Defla. When the British separated Pakistan from India and granted them both independence, Pakistanis renamed cities, streets, and administrative areas; in the northeast, the city of Montgomery—named after Bernard Law, first viscount Montgomery of Alamein, British field marshal and the commander of Allied ground troops during the invasion of Normandy in World War II—reverted to Sahiwal, the previous name for the city and for the Punjab region.

In postcolonial Africa before World War II, there were twelve sovereign states. Today there are almost one hundred, seventeen in France's former colonies alone. Rhodesia, in the former Cape Colony, was created in the 1890s when whites moving north from South Africa met other whites moving southeast as part of the Congo Free State enterprise, launched by King Leopold II of Belgium. Rhodesia got its name from Cecil Rhodes, whose British South Africa Company dominated both the Kimberley diamond mines and the Transvaal gold-mining areas, and who was prime minister from 1890 to 1896. Southern Rhodesia became a self-governing unit of the British Empire in 1923. In 1964, the United Kingdom granted independence to Northern Rhodesia (later Zambia) and Nyasaland (later Malawi). In 1965, Southern Rhodesia declared independence, and in 1970, it renamed itself the State of Rhodesia and renounced allegiance to the British Crown. Writing in 1972, C. M. Matthews predicted the name Rhodesia would survive "because, anomalous though it is, the Rhodesians have broken the political link with England in order to preserve the English tradition they value, and, in standing alone, their loyalties are more concentrated on their own name than before." She was proven wrong just eight years later, when the name Zimbabwe erased the name Rhodesia from the world's maps.

The inhabitants of the kingdom called Basutoland (now Lesotho) are the Basotho, who speak Sesotho. Called Basutoland during the colonial period, at independence in 1966 the country reinstated its correct name. Basuto wasn't simply an English-language alternative; it was simply incorrect.

After the dissolution of the USSR, more than 95 percent of the place-names in Ukraine reverted to pre-Soviet spellings or versions. The country also got rid of the Russian version of its name, Ukrainskaya. Volodymyr Zholdokov, assistant to the ambassador at the Permanent Mission of Ukraine to the United Nations, carefully notes, "We insist on dropping 'the' before 'Ukraine,' for the article implies here [that it is] part of some bigger country, which is not the case."

An undated letter from a Leonid Kapelyushny, published in the Russian newspaper *Izvestia*, sheds light on the issue: "Beginning with 1654, after the merger of the Ukrainian state with the Moscow czardom, there was a consistent policy of wiping out Ukraine as a national state. The Russian empire resembled a python which stifled to half-death a big country, digesting it quietly." On behalf of his fellow Ukrainians, crawling out of the python's jaws three centuries later, reclaiming their heritage and culture, and rejecting Russianization, Kapelyushny explains, "We are not guided by strict calculations, but by biblical morality, affection and emotions." Keep those three factors in mind when you decide what place-names to use.

PRIMAL NAMES

THE PICTORIAL GLOBE

It would be possible to produce a map of the world using the one universal language: pictures. Place-names' etymons (literal meanings of their roots) would offer the perfect guide to the choice of images, as, for example, Brazil's name illustrates. For centuries, European textile makers produced red and purple dye from several species of trees today generically known as "dyewood" trees. When explorers discovered the trees flourishing in South America, they had a ready-made name for the territory: Tierra de Brasil, "land of the brasilwood." The root, *brasa*, means "live coals" or "embers," referring to the color of the wood. This ancient word traveled through the centuries, via the Old Spanish or Old Portuguese *brasil*, then into Middle English as *brasile*.

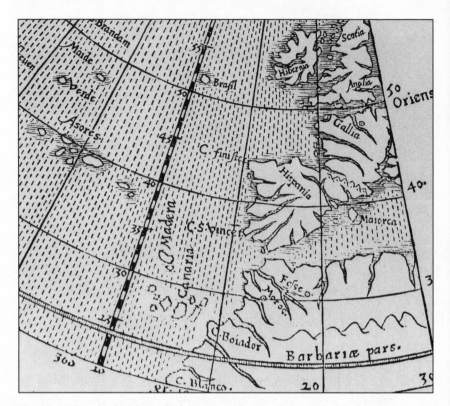

Fig. 41. When the British installed the name Nova Scotia in North America as a replacement for France's Acadia, they were using the old Latin version of Scotland's name, shown on this map along with the Latin name for England. Both names derive from ethnic names: Scotland was Scuit-land, "land of the Scuits," and England was Angle-land, "land of the Angles." (Reproduced from the collections of the Library of Congress.)

The Arctic would be represented by a bear, from the Greek word *arctos*, because Ursa Major, the Great Bear constellation, is most prominent in northern skies. Kuwait would appear as a small fort, from the Arabic word *kout* or *kut*, a house built in the form of a fortress near water. The Maori name for New Zealand is Aotearoa, "land of the long white cloud." Portugal's name comes from the medieval

DEREK NELSON

Latin Portus Cale, "warm harbor": it was free of ice year-round.

Viewed via their etymons, place-names that seem vague and distant to the average reader become vivid and distinct. The Caribbean island of Nevis was once Nuestra Señora de las Nieves, "our lady of the snows." Other names that have a strong, tangible association reveal surprises; coffee doesn't appear on the list of suggested derivations of Java. Instead, toponymists propose rice, millet, *jayah* (nutmegs), or the Sanskrit *java dvipa* (barley island).

Most of the etymons in place-names were inspired by terrain and native plants and animals. Topographic etymons reach back to the elementary stages of civilization, mirroring the simple visual concepts that parents teach young children: size, shape, and color. Large features were a predictable source. In the United States, Michigan comes from *Michigaman*, an Algonquian word meaning "great water," and designated both a tribe and the place where they lived. Mississippi comes from the Chippewa *mice sipi*, "big river." Massachusetts may come from an Algonquian name meaning "place of the big hill," perhaps referring to the Berkshire Hills in the western part of state.

Luxembourg, a fief of the Holy Roman Empire during the mid-1300s, comes from Old Saxon *luttil* (little) and *bu-rug* (town). It developed around a tenth-century castle that, paradoxically for a small town, was one of Europe's strongest fortresses until it was dismantled in 1867. The name of one of its neighbors, the Netherlands, physically describes the country: Old English *nithera*, meaning "lower" or "under." One-quarter of the nation lies below sea level, and only man-made barriers keep the North Sea from flooding coastal regions twice a day. Belgium, Luxembourg, and the Netherlands are widely and aptly known as the Low Countries because of this geography.

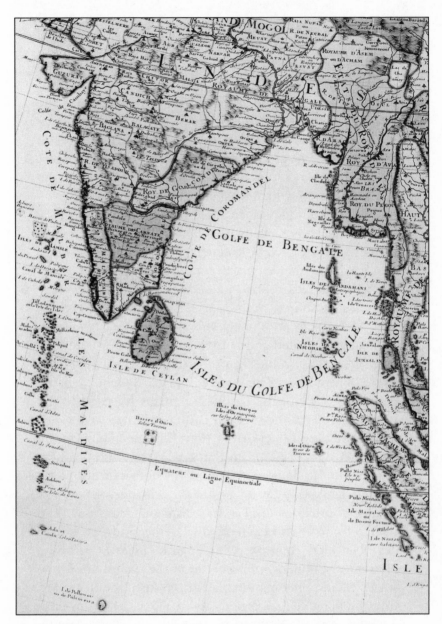

Fig. 42. *The Maldives' name means "thousand islands," but there are actually more than twice that many coral atolls off the coast of India. About one-tenth of them are inhabited. (Reproduced from the collections of the Library of Congress.)*

158

DEREK NELSON

Israelis often refer to the Sea of Galilee, a freshwater lake in northern Israel, as Kinneret (Hebrew for "harp") because of its distinctive outline. Anguilla, northernmost of the Leeward Islands in the West Indies, gets its name from the Latin word for "eel," presumably because its northern coast zig-zags. Sicily, the largest Mediterranean island, was formerly called Trinacria (Greek for "triangle"); some references attribute the name Sicily to the root word *sica*, "sickle." An agrarian tribe named the Siculi or Sekeloi lived in the region during the first century; their name came from a word meaning "reapers," which may in turn link with the tool they used, a sickle.

An old name for Cyprus was Kerastia, "the horned one": the island's shape apparently resembled the stretched hide of a deer. The shape of another animal suggested an ancient name for the Japanese island of Honshu: O-Yamato-toyo-akitsu-shima, "the great Yamato, the fertile island of the dragonfly." A legendary deity bestowed the name after climbing a high mountain and viewing the outline of the island.

An artist couldn't render a pictorial map of the world in black and white. Oklahoma comes from a Choctaw Indian word meaning "red people." The vast Sahara in northern Africa is Sahra in Arabic, from *ashar*, which describes the color of desert sand. The name dates from the ninth century and was long synonymous with desert in European cartography. John Speed's book of maps published in London in 1627 labels it "Sarra which is as much to say as a desert," and a 1727 map of Africa shows "Sahra, ou Le Desert."

The Hebrew name for the Lebanon Mountains, which rise steeply from the coast between Syria and Israel, is *l'banon*, "white mountain"; sources attribute the color to snow or to cliffs of chalk or limestone. Similarly, the bril-

Fig. 43. The Sahara's preeminence as the world's largest sand desert is underscored by the fact that its name is literally synonymous with the word desert in Arabic, and many old maps labeled it as such. (Reproduced from the collections of the Library of Congress.)

liant reflection of light from rivers and lakes in Argentina may have conjured its name, which means "silvery (land)." The name probably originated in the north, where the huge Rio de la Plata, one of the major waterways in the Western Hemisphere, seasonally floods a massive al-

DEREK NELSON

luvial region. Some sources suggest that Sebastian Cabot, who explored South America for Spain between 1526 and 1530, named the Rio de la Plata after the native silver jewelry and ornaments. "Plate" is an old name for silver or gold utensils or dishes. As it happens, the silver probably didn't originate in Argentina but in the Bolivian mountains far to the west.

The rising and setting sun reflected in Lake Malawi (formerly Lake Nyasa) produced the illusion of fire and may have given the country in southeast Africa its name. Kings M. Phiri, a historian at the University of Malawi, traces the name to the Maravi, who migrated from the Luba country in Zaire during the fifteenth century. It may derive from the word for "heat" or "flame" in Chichewa, the Bantu language of the Chewa. (The country endures sweltering heat from September to April, and fires burn continually during the annual ritual incineration of the Marimba bush on the southwestern side of the lake.) The ancient Phoenicians, who inhabited the eastern coast of the Mediterranean in the ninth century B.C., got their name from the Greek word for "purple," because a type of cloth dyed that color was one of their most valuable trade goods.

Many old names came from merchant mariners, whose livelihood (and survival) depended on knowing the coasts and the winds. Some sources trace Macao's name to a Portuguese corruption of the Chinese Ama-ngao, "bay of Ama," named after a goddess worshiped by sailors. Malta, an island in the Mediterranean off Sicily, got its name from the Greek name Melite, which in turn came from a Phoenician word for "shelter" or "refuge (from the sea)." Malta had been a Phoenician and Carthaginian colony when it was captured by the Romans in 218 B.C.

In September 1499, Amerigo Vespucci sailed into an Indian village in South America built on pilings. He named it Venezia (Venice); it later took the name Venezuela, a diminutive form that means "little Venice." The name spread from village to region and became the country's official name in 1830.

A year before Vespucci went to Venezuela, Vasco da Gama sailed around Africa en route to India. He anchored off Mozambique on the southeast coast of Africa, long inhabited by Arab and Swahili traders in gold and ivory. Portuguese commercial settlements would follow in the early 1500s, but harbors were already bustling with fleets of merchant ships. Da Gama recorded a native word, *mosambuco*, "gathering of boats."

Somalia comes from a Cushite word for "dark" or "black," a reference by explorers to skin color. In "Tanzania," which blends former countries Tanganyika and Zanzibar, *zan* comes from Arabic *zang*, "black." Mauritania on the western coast of Africa and the island of Mauritius in the Indian Ocean both derive from the Greek word for black, as does Moor.

The Greeks of Constantinople watched the sun rise over the mountains of Asia Minor and called that land Anatolia (the rising), still the regional name for three-fifths of Turkey. Similarly, a contemporary German word for the Orient is *das Morgenland* (the morning land). Japan's name summons yet another eternal dawn. In 671, the Chinese gave a name variously written as Jin-Pen or Jeupenn to the archipelago east of their empire. It meant "(land of the) rising sun." The Japanese adopted the name, modifying its pronunciation to Nihon, *ni* meaning "sun" and *hon* meaning "source" or "origin." The countries of the eastern Mediterranean—Greece, Turkey, Syria, Jordan, and Egypt—came to be known as the Levant (which means "rising up"), because, viewed from Italy, that is where the sun appears to rise. When Syria and Lebanon were included in

DEREK NELSON

Fig. 44. *Some places are named not by their inhabitants but by their neighbors. Anatolia (here written as Natolia) is the Asian part of Turkey, usually synonymous with Asia Minor. The name derives from the Greek word for sunrise, because Turkey was to its east. (Reproduced from the collections of the Library of Congress.)*

a French mandate established by the Treaty of Sèvres, they were called the Levant States.

Österreich, "eastern kingdom" (its relative position in a larger state), was used as early as November 1, 996, in a court document. It was superseded in 1147 by the Latin version, Austria, which gained widespread use because of Latin's role as a global language in the Middle Ages.

Norway's name is even older than Austria's. It derives from the Norse Nordvegr, "northern way," and originally referred to one of the three main sea routes to and from Scandinavia. The name came to denote the coast and, by the ninth century, the territory approximating modern Norway.

Australia was on the bottom of many medieval maps of

the world; the name derives from Auster, the personification of the south wind. A 1763 map of the Southern Hemisphere labels the continent "Southern Land." Vietnam comes from an ancient Chinese name, Ywet Nam, "(territory) south of Yueh." Yueh was an area in southern China now encompassing the provinces of Kwangtung, Fukien, Chekiang, and Kiangsi.

In the center of European world maps was the Mediterranean, the "ocean in the middle of the land." The Romans called it Mare Nostrum, "our sea." The Japanese name for the Mediterranean, Chichukai, is a literal translation of the meaning. The German version is das Mittelmeer, the "central sea." An unusual version of the name appears in the aforementioned 1627 London book of maps: On Hudson Bay is the legend "This Westmediterranean Sea was first found by Mr. Hudson."

The Gobi Desert stretches east to west from southeastern Mongolia to northern China. A series of shallow alkaline basins at elevations ranging from 3,000 to 5,000 feet, it is raked by fierce winds and sandstorms from the northwest. The winds have stripped away most of the soil, producing the source of the Gobi's name, a Mongolian word meaning "gravel and rock debris." Botswana's Kalahari Desert, 100,000 square miles of grassland and dense scrub in southwest Africa, is physically less severe than the Gobi, but the meaning of its name is more forbidding: the "great thirstland." A suggested derivation of the name Arabia is the Arabic *arabah*, "waste" or "barren wilderness"; the southern interior of Saudi Arabia contains a vast desert named Rub al-Khali, "the empty quarter."

One expects deserts to be barren and bodies of water to be fecund. But near the present-day Israel-Jordan border, Romans found an inland sea that seemed the Rub al-Khali's liquid counterpart, devoid of animals and plants.

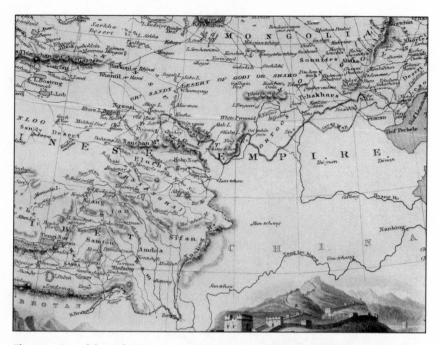

Fig. 45. *Part of the Gobi Desert's Mandarin name* (Yintai Shamo) *appears on this 1851 map. More than twice the size of the Rub al-Khali, the Gobi is known for its cold winters and short, hot summers, raked throughout the year by fierce winds and sand-storms. Its name means "gravel and rock debris." (Reproduced from the collections of the Library of Congress.)*

They accurately named it Mare Mortum, the "dead sea." Its waters are 26 percent salt (most oceans are 3 or 4 percent) and support no visible life. The coast is the lowest dry point on earth, 1,292 feet below sea level. The Dead Sea is more than four times farther below sea level than the lowest point in the Western Hemisphere, Death Valley in the American Southwest. But the Dead Sea's lively history belies its name. Sodom and Gomorrah, the definitive biblical dens of iniquity, were on the southwest shore, and the Dead Sea Scrolls were discovered in caves on the northwest shore in 1947.

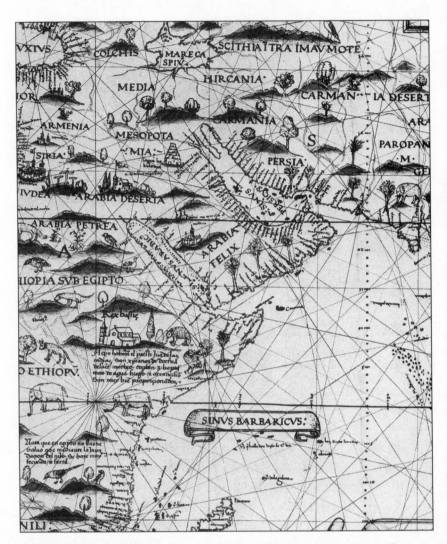

Fig. 46. *If Arabia's name derives from the Arabic* arabah, *meaning "waste" or "barren wilderness," then the name Arabia Felix is oxymoronic, because the Latin* felix *means "happy." This section of the Arabian peninsula was sometimes labeled with that name because it isn't a desert. (Reproduced from the collections of the Library of Congress.)*

DEREK NELSON

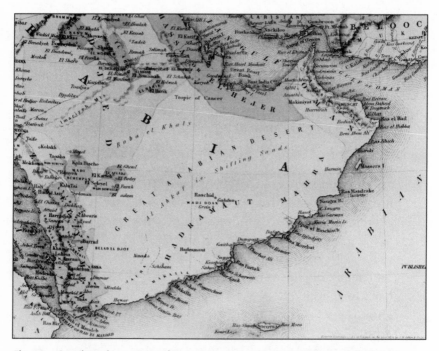

Fig. 47. *Desolate places attract descriptive names. The 225,000-square-mile Rub al-Khali (whose name means "empty quarter") on the Arabian peninsula features 660-foot sand dunes. (Reproduced from the collections of the Library of Congress.)*

To find the earth's highest point, travel 3,000 miles east and 5 miles up, to the peaks of the Himalaya. The name derives from the Sanskrit *hima* (snow) and *alaja* (an abode). The 1,500-mile mountain chain formed as the earth's crust folded against the Indian subcontinent, shoved northward by tectonic plates. The mountains run from Pakistan through India, Tibet, Nepal, and into Bhutan. Although thirty of the peaks soar higher than 25,000 feet, only one of three ranges, the Great Himalaya in the north, is blanketed with snow year-round.

At least a dozen place-names are represented by rivers on the pictorial globe. Peru was named by the Spanish in the sixteenth century after a river, Biru, whose name in turn may derive from an Indian word for "river" or from the name of a tribal chief whose realm was in extreme northwest South America, next to the Isthmus of Darien. Nebraska's name comes from the Omaha Indian name Nibthaska, "river in the flatness," referring to the Platte River (whose name, incidentally, comes from the French word for "flat"). Niger comes from the local word *n'eghirren*, "flowing water." The river describes a large northeastern arc through western Africa, a geographic oddity that made it mysterious to Europeans, who long confused it with the Nile and the Congo—the continent's two larger rivers—helping make Tombouctou, on the Niger in Mali, synonymous with remoteness.

The etymology of the Ivory Coast may reach all the way back to the Egyptian word *abu*, meaning both "elephant" and "ivory." An elephant appears on the nation's coat of arms. Trade in elephant tusks flourished there in the late nineteenth and early twentieth centuries, by which time the species had been pushed near extinction.

The name of Mali, the Ivory Coast's neighbor to the south, may come from a Mandingo word that means "hippopotamus." The lower part of the country is in the flood plain of the Niger, where hippos still bask. Cameroon, in western Africa on the Gulf of Guinea, gets its name from the Portuguese word for shrimp, *camarao*, which were apparently abundant in its coastal waters.

Singapore derives from the Sanskrit *simha* or *singa* (lion) and *pur* or *pura* (city). A Malayan chronicle records the thirteenth-century encounter of a Sumatran prince with what was probably a tiger, but which he recorded as being a lion; both animals now appear on the country's coat of arms. The event produced the name Singapura.

Spanish explorers named the Caribbean island of Barbados by using the Spanish word for "bearded." They were struck, according to various sources, by the tangle of thick vines, the streamers of moss hanging from the trees, or the Indian fig trees on the island. The name of a nearby island, Barbuda, reportedly refers to long beards worn by the natives.

The Madeira Islands, off the coast of Morocco, got their name from trees. The source was a Portuguese translation of the Italian word for "timber," referring to dense forests. Switzerland's name derives from lack of same: "Schwyz" from *suedan*, an old German word that meant "to burn," referred to a forest that had been cleared by burning.

Mexico's name also commemorates a feature now absent: a lake that stood on the present site of Mexico City. Aztecs had called it Metzlianan, from *metz-li*, "moon" (to which it was dedicated) and *atl*, "water." The name later became Metz-xih-co, "in the center (literally, 'navel') of the waters of the moon," and gradually spread to the entire territory.

The current brochure published by the Board on Geographic Names instructs those who wish to name a previously anonymous feature on the American landscape or rename a place: "New names should be imaginative and distinctive. The Board prefers names descriptive of topographic forms . . . or names associated with natural life or other phenomena." The globe is full of such names. Perhaps they are the best of all: durable, apolitical, and rooted in the earth itself.

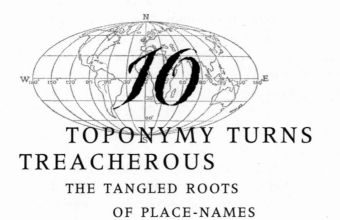

TOPONYMY TURNS
TREACHEROUS
THE TANGLED ROOTS
OF PLACE-NAMES

Blackheath is a residential district in southeast London where golf was introduced to England in 1608. "Heath" comes from an old English word meaning "uncultivated land"; and surely "black" means the opposite of white. Well, maybe not. The first syllable of the name might come from the Norse *blakka*, "white." The name could date from the Viking invasions of the late eighth century, as do a host of other British place-names.

Until the Middle Ages in Europe, names were often based on landscape, location, or another aspect of geography. Nepal's name, for example, comes from a Sanskrit word that means "abode at the foot" (of the Himalaya); Ukraine derives from the Slavonic *krai*, "boundary" or "frontier." During the fifteenth and sixteenth centuries, Spanish and Portuguese missionaries, settlers, and explorers deposited hundreds of religious names around the globe (those preceded by the word *Saint* fill fourteen pages of *Webster's New Geographical Dictionary*). From the seventeenth through the nineteenth centuries, French, English, and Dutch explorers added names commemorating people or homeland: Mauritius in honor of Prince Maurice of Orange, the governor of Holland and Zeeland, who led the Netherlands' struggle for independence from Spain in the early 1600s; New Jersey after the largest of the Channel Islands, named by Sir George Carteret (a native of the isle of Jersey and an early holder of the royal land grant to that region of the colonies).

If all place-names fell into one of these broad genres, toponymy would be easy, but gazetteers are spiced with exceptions and anomalies. For every Rhode Island (from the Dutch Roodt Eylandt, "red island," after the local clay) there is a Red Sea. The name, which doesn't describe the color of the water, is said to have referred to the skin color of the Semitic people who lived on the shores, and who may have appeared reddish compared to ethnic groups whose skin looked black or yellow. Describing the skin of Semitic people as "red" is unusual, but this tenuous explanation will survive until someone offers a better one.

Toponymy is a chronically imprecise endeavor, a blend of theory and educated guess. Careful researchers take refuge in the indefinite. According to O. D. von Engeln and Jane Urquhart, authors of the 1924 *Story Key to Geographic Names*, Uruguay was supposedly named after a bird with remarkable tail feathers, but the "bird's tail" was actually a local waterfall. Adrian Room echoes their explanation, saying that *uru* means "bird" and *guay* means "tail" in an unspecified Indian language; however, he points out, *guay* might mean "river." In *Geographical Etymology*, C. Blackie wrote in 1887 that Paraguay comes from the Brazilian *para* (river, water, or the sea) and that the country's name means "the place of waters" (which implies that *guay* means "place"). Von Engeln and Urquhart offer *Paraguacu*, "great water," without identifying the language. George Stewart, author of several standard references, identifies the language as Guarani and writes that *guay* derives from *guaso*, "big." He adds that another local word might be the origin: *paragua*, which means "crown of feathers."

Panamá, according to the staff at the country's United Nations Mission, means either "many fish" or "abundance of butterflies." In *Names on the Globe*, Stewart traces the former explanation to the sixteenth-century chronicler Bartolomé de las Casas, and Room notes that Spanish explorers found many fishermen's huts during their sixteenth-century visits. Taylor suggests that Panamá was named after mud fish, and "Panama Bay, the bay of mud fish" is in the index of Blackie's book.

Some sources think that Spain derives from the Phoenician *sapan* or *span*, which describes the skin of the marten, a weasel-like carnivore. Spain was reportedly a source of these furs, which, like mink and ermine pelts, have been a prized part of apparel since medieval times. Other possible derivations are an old Spanish word for rabbit; the Basque *ezpana*, "shore"; and a root word connected to mining: The first colonists in Spain—Phoenicians, Greeks, and Carthaginians—aimed to establish a base for trade and gain access to mineral resources, such as the iron and coal mines in the Cantabrian Mountains.

Ethiopia is perhaps an adaptation of the like-sounding Egyptian Ethaush, although the Egyptian name for Ethiopians was Habashat, which is probably the origin of Ethiopia's former name, Abyssinia. Another, more commonly accepted theory is that Ethiopia was a Greek name, derived from *aithein*, "to burn," plus *ops*, "countenance." The name, therefore, described the complexion of the inhabitants.

David Hernandez, a teacher in Belmopan, the capital of Belize, probed local geographic and ethnic history to arrive at the origin of the country's name. His search led him first to dispose of a standard Mexican explanation: that Belize came from the French *balise*, "beacon." The early settlers, buccaneers hostile to the French, were likely neither to adopt a word from the language nor to erect or tolerate a beacon marking their lair. The usual English explanation of the name is that it was a corruption of the name of a Scottish sea captain or pirate named Peter Wallace (or Willis), who allegedly established a camp at the mouth of the Belize River in 1640. Camp and river became known as Wally's or Willie's, which the Spanish mispronounced. Eighteenth- century maps and accounts spelled it Wallix, Valys, Bullys, Bellise, and Belice. Colonial administrations in Belize opted for the Wallace theory in order to document the primacy of European influence. Hernandez found no documentation linking anyone named Wallace or Willis to Belize. He did find a circumstantial connection with pirates from Tortuga, an island on which Wallace's doings are well-documented. However, Wallace disappears from the historical record before his supposed arrival on Belize.

The country's first self-governing administration rejected this theory, calling attention to "the unbroken Mayan heritage of this land" by suggesting that Belize was a corruption of the Mayan Belakin (land to the east) or Beliz (muddy water). Hernandez found these proposals as unconvincing as the Wallace theory and took his research, instead, into a previously unexplored direction. He knew

174

that slaves began arriving in Belize in the early eighteenth century, often bringing names that they assigned to local places and taught to later arrivals. Studying old African maps, Hernandez discovered a tiny village named Belize in the Cabinda Province of Angola.

Canary birds originated in the Canary Islands, a group of Spanish islands in the Atlantic off the northwest coast of Africa, but the islands weren't named for them. The Spanish name Islas Canarias is from the Latin Canariae Insulae, "isles of dogs." The name originated with sailors who heard barking on the shore.

Like the name Blackheath, the Amazon River would seem to be an easy name to pin down. Is there any doubt that the name of the world's second largest river leaped from mythology to map? When the Spanish explorer Francisco de Orellana voyaged downstream from a northern tributary in 1541, a tribe called the Tapuyas attacked his crew. De Orellana reported that Tapuya women fought alongside men, although historians now think he may have mistaken long-haired men for women. His reports were convincingly reminiscent of the legendary tribe of warlike women who lived in Asia Minor. According to Greek myth, the Amazons fought with the Trojans under a queen who was later killed by Achilles.

In fact, the river's name probably derived from a local word for the river. One source renders it *amazunu* or *amassunu*, "big wave," describing the violent tidal bore in its lower reaches. Another cites *amassona*, "boat destroyer." De Orellana or other contemporary visitors may have misunderstood the word and taken it as confirming the identity of the local tribe they'd fought.

The old Roman name for Ireland—Hibernia—has often been wrongly attributed to the Latin *hibernus*, "wintry."

Fig. 48. *The pitfalls of toponymy are illustrated by the name Hibernia, the ancient Latin name for Ireland (top right). The logical association is with the Latin root of words such as "hibernate," perhaps denoting Ireland's colder climate compared to that of the sunny Mediterranean. Actually, the name came from Celtic and Greek roots, sometimes translated as "country of the warriors." (Reproduced from the collections of the Library of Congress.)*

The name actually came from old Celtic and Greek roots: *ibh*, "country" or "people," and *erna*, "of the nobles" or "of the warriors." Some etymologists trace the latter root to the Sanskrit *arya*, "noble," which also appears in the name Iran.

Sun-kissed Florida might seem to mean "flowery land" because of its lush vegetation, but the derivation is indirect. Juan Ponce de León discovered it on Easter Sunday, which the Spaniards call Pascua Florida, because of the flowers that decorate churches on that day.

If you look for Bermuda on some seventeenth- and eighteenth-century maps, you'll find it labeled Summer Islands. Bermuda comes from Spanish navigator Juan de Bermudez, reputedly the first European to either land on or sail past the islands, sometime between 1503 and 1511. The islands were uninhabited when British admiral Sir George Somers (chartered as a prospective deputy-governor by the Virginia Company of London) and a group of five hundred colonists were briefly shipwrecked there en route to Virginia in July 1609. Somers later died during a return trip to Bermuda, and the British renamed Bermuda in his honor. The name gradually changed into Summer Islands when later mapmakers took it as a reference to the climate.

A particularly colorful folk legend grew out of the name of Antwerp, Belgium's largest port, located on the Schelde River. The city was a commercial and trading center as early as the fifteenth century. The name derives from the Dutch *aan*, "at," and *werf*, "wharf." However, a much more dramatic local story revolves around its derivation from the Flemish *handt werper*, "hand throwing." Whenever strangers refused to pay the toll at the Schelde, an ogre named Antigonus cut off their right hands and tossed them into the river as punishment. This tale circulated as early

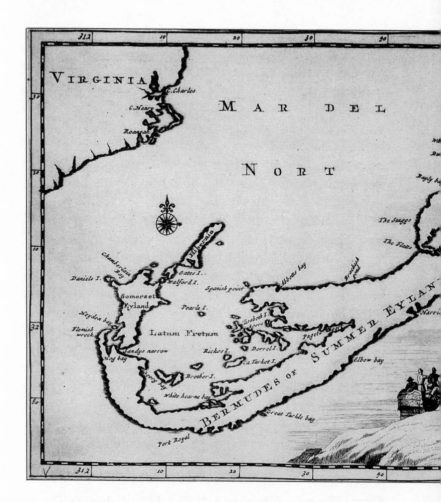

as the 1630s and became so well accepted that the city's crest in the late 1800s showed two severed hands.

The Reverend Isaac Taylor recounts a similar story about an English town originally named Leighton Beau-désert (*beau* in French means "beautiful" or "handsome," and désert, "solitary place," clearing in a forest," or "wilderness"). This elegant Gallic name was gradually anglicized to Leighton Buzzard. Noticing a golden bird carved on the

DEREK NELSON

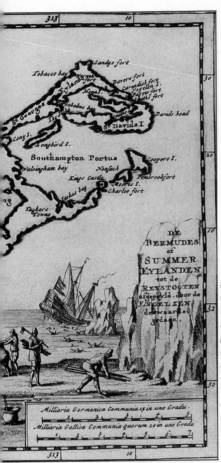

Fig. 49. *English naval commander Sir George Somers claimed Bermuda for England after being shipwrecked there. Several versions of the shipwreck were published at the time; Somers's adventure may have even suggested a story line for Shakespeare's* The Tempest. *But even though the incident was well-known at the time, Somers's name was nevertheless corrupted to "Summers" during later centuries, and further misinterpreted as a reference to a season and to Bermuda's climate. (Reproduced from the collections of the Library of Congress.)*

lectern in the parish church, a town sexton decided that it must be the buzzard (it was an eagle). Visitors were henceforth treated to this documentation of the origin of the town's name.

The Mexican city of Tijuana sometimes appears as Tia Juana, a version some dictionaries accept as the "old Spanish spelling." Residents of San Diego, California, just north of Tijuana, have used Tia Juana and have even erected street signs with that version. Local Spanish speakers and others clearly pronounce the name with a "tia" sound. One assumes then, that the name is from *tia Juana*, "aunt Jane." Instead, it derives from the Amerindian *tiwana*, "by the sea."

Similar misunderstandings, alleged or otherwise, have generated a genre of comical etymologies that crop up in reference books, sometimes offered seriously. The name Guinea is occasionally said to have derived from Portuguese seafarers who went ashore and asked the name of the place. Locals thought they were pointing at a group of nearby women and answered, *"Guine"* (women). The capital of Gambia, West Africa, was named Bathurst after a British colonial secretary in the early 1800s. It was officially changed in 1973 to Banjul, which local people were already using. Portuguese settlers in the fifteenth century asked what the place was called, and their question was misunderstood as "What are you doing?" "Bangjulo," came the reply: "Making rope mats."

A French explorer surveying the desolate Canadian countryside is supposed to have sighed, *"Ca nada,"* which means "Here is nothing" in Portuguese. He would hardly have complained in Portuguese. Canada's name, as we have seen, actually comes from the Iroquois *kanata*, "collection of huts."

Such tales are easily debunked. Most riddles in toponymy are more elaborate. Does the name Chile come from the Quichua Indian word *chiri*, meaning "cold," or from the Nahuatl Indian word *chilli*, the incendiary peppers of the plant *Capsicum frutescens?* The Quichua language was spoken by Indians in western Guatemala who were related to the ancient Maya. Nahuatl is derived from ancient Aztec and is spoken today mainly in Mexico. Neither language has ever been spoken in Chile, and neither Central American country is Chile's neighbor. Both derivations are suspect. Advocates of the first trace the name to Peruvian Incas, who found Chile's climate cool compared to their equatorial homeland. But George Stewart cites the sixteenth-century Spanish chronicler Antonio de Herrera y Tordesillas as saying that a river named Chile existed before Inca times. *Chili* does mean "hot pepper" in Spanish, and the plant was cultivated in South America before Columbus. Chili peppers, however, are associated much more strongly with Mexican cooking.

In the 1987 *Historical Dictionary of Chile*, Salvatore Bizzarro explains that the name comes from a Chilean thrush called a *trile*, which during flight "emits the sound 'chi-li, chi-li.'" Von Engeln and Urquhart agreed with this derivation, dismissing the "cold" theory because it seemed "too much like English to be believable." But place-name references, in general, are fraught with such believable theories. Likely stories endure because people like them.

A TOUCH OF
SERENDIPITY

In April 1999, Canada will have a new province, Nunavut, made up of the eastern part of the Northwest Territories; the indigenous Inuit will thereby assume political control over a fifth of the country. The 750,000-square-mile territory will extend north from Hudson and Baffin Bays to the Arctic Ocean and Greenland. The name, appropriately, means "our land."

Perhaps the Ambonese Christians in Indonesia, a mainly Muslim country, will gain independence for the neighboring South Moluccan islands, triggering the need for a new place-name. Extremist Sikhs in India want a state called Khalistan; Kanaks (Melanesians) in New Caledonia have violently agitated for independence from France since the mid-1980s, envisioning a country called Kanaky, which has yet to materialize.

Will Macao get a new name after it becomes a special administrative region under Chinese sovereignty in 1999? The Chinese government may require a symbolic assertion of their authority. The name Macao derives from the Ma Kwok temple, built in the fourteenth century. Portuguese merchants established a trading post there in 1557, and as an overseas province of Portugal, it was called the Portuguese Asian Dependency.

In the years to come, many familiar names may change. Mount McKinley in Alaska, the highest point in North America, might finally be renamed Denali, an old Athabaskan Indian name that has far more local significance. (The name of Mount McKinley National Park was changed to Denali National Park in 1980, a step in that direction.) Other indigenous names will also battle their way back onto world maps. A current Japanese atlas lists, along with the name Bangkok, the local name Krung Thep (capital of the angels). Will English-language maps follow suit?

Meander comes from the Menderes River in Phrygia in Asia Minor. The name now applies to several rivers in Turkey, the most important being the Buyuk Menderes in the southwestern part of the country. It runs east-west, twisting and turning for 250 miles on its way to the Aegean Sea at Miletus. Actually, it doesn't seem to meander any more than most other rivers, certainly no more than the mighty Mississippi.

Long before Sri Lanka was known as Ceylon, the Romans called it Sarandib or Serendip, a name that appears in the title of a Persian fairy tale called (in English) "The Three Princes of Serendip." The princes had an aptitude for accidentally making fortunate discoveries; English writer Horace Walpole coined *serendipity* in 1754 to describe the phenomenon.

The earth-based roots of two cities with glamorous cosmopolitan histories, London and Paris, are revealed by the etymology of their names. London originated as a harbor in the Thames between two bleak, rocky hills; the name derives from the Celtic *long*, "the wild place." Paris, the famous moveable feast, started out as a bad place for a picnic. The name comes from the Latin Lutetia Parisianorum, "mud flats of the Parisi." The Parisi were a Gallic tribe whose Celtic ancestors invaded France in the fourth and third centuries B.C. Romans used the Latin name when they occupied the one-time fishing village. The Latin name appears on Ptolemy's maps.

Alaska collected several sarcastic nicknames—Seward's Icebox, Seward's Folly, Icebergia, and Walrussia—before the virtues of the 600,000-square-mile addition to the United States became apparent. The Seward in question was William Henry Seward, secretary of state under President Andrew Johnson, Lincoln's successor. Even before the Civil War, overtures had been made toward buying what was then called Russian America. Seward arranged the purchase in 1867, convincing the Russian ambassador to reduce the original $10 million asking price by 30 percent. The treaty was negotiated and drafted in a single night and was signed before the House of Representatives voted the appropriation. Seward chose the territory's name himself; it comes from the Aleut A-la-as-ka, "the great country."

Place-names change, but related words remain in our vocabulary. Siamese cats will still stretch out on Persian rugs for afternoon naps, and painters will still squeeze Prussian blue on their palettes, even though the place names commemorated in these modifiers vanished in the 1930s and 1940s.

When we choose and use place-names, logic will not

prevail. English speakers will continue to use the Swedish version of Finland's name, and Swedes will keep using the German version of France's name. It would be nice to call everyone by their own name, but that is a utopian notion. The English statesman and author Sir Thomas More conceived Utopia in a book by that name in 1516, describing an imaginary country with ideal laws and social conditions. Inevitably, the name comes from the Greek *ou*, meaning "no" or "not," plus *topos*, "place": nowhere.

BIBLIOGRAPHY

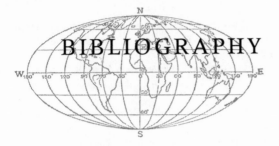

Adams, Percy G. *Travelers and Travel Liars 1660–1800*. Berkeley: University of California Press, 1962.

Aurousseau, M. *The Rendering of Geographical Names*. 1957. Reprint, Westport, Conn.: Greenwood Press, 1975.

Betteridge, Harold, ed. *The New Cassell's German Dictionary*. New York: Funk & Wagnalls, 1971.

Birmingham, David, and Phyllis Martin, eds. *History of Central Africa*, Vol. 3. London and New York: Longman, 1983.

Bizzarro, Salvatore. *Historical Dictionary of Chile*. Metuchen, N.J.: Scarecrow Press, 1987.

Blackie, C[hristina]. *Geographical Etymology: A Dictionary of Place-Names Giving Their Derivations*. London: Murray, 1887.

Bobb, F. Scott. *Historical Dictionary of Zaire*. Metuchen, N.J.: Scarecrow Press, 1988.

Boyd, Andrew. *An Atlas of World Affairs*. London: Methuen, 1987.

Brown, Lloyd A. *The Story of Maps*. New York: Bonanza Books, 1949.

Century Dictionary and Cyclopedia. Vol. 12, *Cyclopedia of Names*. New York: Century, 1911.

Dathorne, O. R. *Imagining the World: Mythical Belief versus Reality in Global Encounters.* Westport, Conn.: Bergin & Garvey, 1994.

Demko, George. *Why in the World: Adventures in Geography.* New York: Doubleday, 1992.

Hammond International World Atlas. Maplewood, N.J.: Hammond, 1975.

Hart, Henry, H. *Sea Road to the Indies.* London: William Hodge, 1952.

Hendrickson, Robert. *The Facts on File Encyclopedia of Word and Phrase Origins.* New York: Facts on File, 1987.

Holmes, Nigel. *Pictorial Maps.* New York: Watson-Guptill, 1991.

Junichi, Natori. *A Short History of Nippon.* Tokyo: Hokuseido Press, 1943.

Lister, Raymond. *Antique Maps and Their Cartographers.* London: G. Bell & Sons, 1970.

Masuda, Koh, ed. *New Japanese-English Dictionary.* Tokyo: Kenkyusha, 1974.

Matthews, C. M. *Place Names of the English-Speaking World.* New York: Scribner, 1972.

Monmonier, Mark. *Drawing the Line: Tales of Maps and Cartocontroversy.* New York: Henry Holt, 1995.

―――. *How to Lie with Maps.* Chicago: University of Chicago Press, 1991.

National Geographic Atlas of the World. Washington, D.C.: National Geographic Society, 1992.

Nelson, Andrew. *The Modern Reader's Japanese-English Dictionary.* Tokyo: Charles E. Tuttle, 1962.

New York Public Library Writer's Guide to Style and Usage. New York: Stonesong Press, 1994.

Palmer, A. Smythe. *Folk-Etymology: A Dictionary of Verbal Corruptions or Words Perverted in Form or Meaning by False Derivation or Mistaken Analogy.* 1883. Reprint, New York: Greenwood Press, 1969.

Papinot, E. *Historical and Geographical Dictionary of Japan.* 1910. Reprint, Ann Arbor, Mich.: Overbeck, 1948.

Peters, Arno. *Peters Atlas of the World.* New York: Harper & Row, 1990.

Pohl, Federick J. *Amerigo Vespucci, Pilot Major.* New York: Columbia University Press, 1944.

Ramsay, Raymond. *No Longer on the Map: Discovering Places That Never Were.* New York: Viking Press, 1972.

Rand McNally Cosmopolitan World Atlas. Chicago: Rand McNally, 1981.

Room, Adrian. *Place-Name Changes Since 1900: A World Gazetteer.* Metuchen, N.J.: Scarecrow Press, 1979.

―――. *Place-Names of the World.* Newton Abbot, England: David & Charles, 1974.

Senior, Olive. *A–Z of Jamaican Heritage*. Portsmouth, N.H.: Heine-
mann, 1983.

Shirley, Rodney. *The Mapping of the World: Early Printed World Maps,
1472–1700*. London: Holland Press, 1983.

Showers, Victor. *World Facts and Figures*. New York: Wiley, 1979.

Skelton, R. A. *Explorers' Maps: Chapters in the Cartographic Record of
Geographical Discovery*. London: Spring Books, 1958.

Stewart, George R. *American Place-Names*. New York: Oxford University Press, 1970.

———. *Names on the Globe*. New York: Oxford University Press, 1975.

———. *Names on the Land*. New York: Random House, 1945.

Taylor, Isaac. *Words and Places; or Etymological Illustrations of History,
Ethnology and Geography*. London: G. Routledge & Sons, 1909.

Thrower, Norman. *Maps & Man: An Examination of Cartography in Re-
lation to Culture and Civilization*. Englewood Cliffs, N.J.: Prentice-
Hall, 1972.

Times Atlas of the World. New York: Times Books, 1985.

Tooley, R. V. *Maps and Map-Makers*. London: B. T. Batsford, 1970.

von Engeln, O. D., and Jane Urquhart. *The Story Key to Geographic
Names*. Port Washington, N.Y.: Kennikat Press, 1970.

Webster's New Geographical Dictionary. Springfield, Mass.: Merriam-
Webster, 1988.

Wood, Denis. *The Power of Maps*. New York: Guilford Press, 1992.

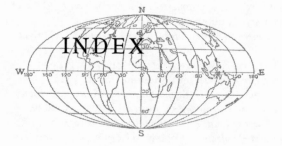

INDEX

Frobisher, Sir Martin, 57–58, 81
Frontenac, Comte de, 101
Fujian, variations of, 127

Gama, Vasco da, 12, 50, 55, 132,
    162
Gambia, 48, 180
Gandhi, Mohandas K., 31
Gaza Strip, 20
Genoese, 52, 92
Georgia, 29
Germany, 14, 22, 30, 43, 92, 95,
    113, 134, 135; language, 28,
    86, 129, 132–34, 139, 141,
    143, 144, 146, 162, 164, 169,
    186; map, 123; variations of,
    132, 142
Ghana, 107
Giles, Herbert, 126
Giovanni (priest), 45
Gobi Desert, 164; variation of,
    165
Golan Heights (Israel), 20, 21
Gold Coast. See Ghana.
Golden Bay, variations of, 83
Grain Coast, 107
Granada, 111
Great Britain. See Britain.
Greece (Greeks), 6, 11, 16, 23–
    24, 30–31, 39, 81, 96, 97, 109,
    162, 173; language, 53, 71, 90,
    121, 124, 126, 156, 159, 161–
    63, 177, 180, 186; myths, 45,
    46, 175
Greenland, 8, 17, 64, 78, 79–82,
    86; variations of, 18, 81, 132,
    152
Grenadines, the, 84
Guadeloupe, 93
Guarani language, 173
Guatemala, 107, 180
Guerard, Albert L., 24, 119
Guiana, 61
Guinea, 108, 180; variation of,
    130
Gulag Archipelago (Russia), 29
Guyana, 21–22
Guyotville (Algeria), variation of,
    153
Gypsies, 90–91

Haiti, 131
Hamburg, 97
Hawaii, 82, 131
Hebrew language, 122, 159
Henry, Patrick, 151
Henry the Navigator, Prince, 11–
    12, 48, 49
Hernandez, David, 174–75
Herrera y Tordesillas, Antonio de,
    181
Himalayan Mountain, 167, 171
Hindus, 6–7
Hispaniola island, 55; variations
    of, 130
Ho Chi Minh, 149–50
Hog Island, 83–84
Holland, 77; variations of, 132.
    See also Dutch; Netherlands.
Holyhead, variation of, 25
Homem, Diogo, 48
Homer, 6
Honan, variation of, 127
Hong Kong, 5
Honshu, variation of, 159
Hottentots, the, 118, 119
Hudson, Henry, 58, 164
Hudson Bay, 58, 164
Hungary, 14, 97, 143; language,
    144, 146; variations of, 123,
    142

Iceland, 81; variation of, 121
Al-Idrisi, As-Sharif, 42–43
Incas, the, 181
India, 6–7, 12, 13, 26, 31–32, 38,
    44, 45, 47, 54, 55, 59, 64, 90,
    104, 149, 153, 158, 162, 167,
    183; variation of, 144
Indian Ocean, 12, 23, 39, 50, 51,
    52, 107
Indies, the, 12, 38, 54, 58, 60, 62,
    79, 104, 105
Indochina, variation of, 55
Indonesia, 105, 183
Insule Martini, 114
International Map of the World,
    134, 135
Internet, 133
Iran, 177
Iraq, 38

195

199

INDEX